101 things
you can do to become an
outstanding
young adult

By David C. Mammano

NextStepU
Rochester, New York

NextStepU.com

NextStepU
2 W. Main St., Suite 200
Victor, NY 14564

Copyright © Next Step Publishing

All rights reserved. No part of this book may be reproduced without written permission from the publisher, except for brief quotations in critical reviews or articles.

For ordering information, call (800) 771-3117 ext. 10 or visit NextStepU.com.

Editor: Laura Jeanne Hammond
Designer: Diana Fisher
Illustrations: McMillan Digital Art
Cover photo: AbleStock.com

Printed and produced in the United States of America.

ISBN: 978-0-9752926-1-7

Introduction

Have you ever wished there were more shortcuts in life? Well, I have news for you: There aren't any. You'll always have to work hard to achieve true success. Don't be discouraged—the journey to success is the most rewarding one you'll ever take! And the best part is that it's never really over.

Success comes from within. Sure your friends may have material things given to them at the drop of a hat. Maybe you do, too. But things do not bring success. It's not what you own on the outside; it's what you become on the inside that really counts.

To be successful, a person needs to have a plan, a strategy for life. Success doesn't just happen by accident. Success happens when a person purposefully integrates certain habits into his or her life. The trick is to make these habits stick. Humans are infamous for starting new habits only to retreat to the old ones in a couple of weeks.

Successful people develop successful habits and stick with them. Repetition is the mother of all skills. Once you master a habit, it becomes part of your life. After a while, you'll perform that successful habit without even thinking about it! It will become your natural reflex.

The earlier you develop those successful

habits, the better. That's why I wrote *101 Things You Can Do to Become an Outstanding Young Adult*—to help you master these skills now.

The closest thing you'll ever find to a "shortcut" in life is this book. Learning these habits will put you on the path to lifelong success. Incorporate these habits into your life, and you'll be well on your way to becoming an outstanding young adult.

Success has nothing to do with your parents' wealth, your intelligence or winning the lottery. It all comes down to your habits and decisions. It's not rocket science. You either make the decision to become outstanding or you don't. If you do decide that you'd like to become outstanding, you will implement good habits into your everyday life.

In many horse races, the first-place horse wins by only a nose. But the difference between first and second place may be a million dollars. By integrating successful habits into your life, you can be like the horse that wins by a nose. By making the decision to become outstanding, you can have the extra advantage it takes to lead the pack.

There is nothing more satisfying than enjoying the fruits of your good habits. You'll develop outstanding character and abilities. You'll find that if you have confidence in your character and abilities, you'll sleep soundly.

I hope you enjoy reading *101 Things You Can Do to Become an Outstanding Young Adult*! When you feel your habits slipping, read it again. Hey, even a grand piano needs to be tuned every so often!

As founder of NextStepU, which helps high school students with college, career and life planning, I encourage you to stay in touch! Let me know how this book has helped you! I can always be reached through NextStepU.com.

And remember, first we make our habits— then our habits make us.

Now go become outstanding!

All my best,

David C. Mammano

David Mammano
David@NextStepU.com

Dedication

I'd like to dedicate this book to my son, Gianluca, and my daughter, Melania.

They already embody all of these 101 lessons! OK, maybe that's just a proud father talking. But seriously, their entrance into this world has been the best thing to ever happen to my wife, Luisa, and me. I can only pray that they will take to heart the lessons from this book and become outstanding young adults.

1. Stop thinking about just yourself,
and volunteer.

You'll feel good, help others and build
your résumé at the same time.

2. Have respect for others and for yourself.

3. Become an expert public speaker.

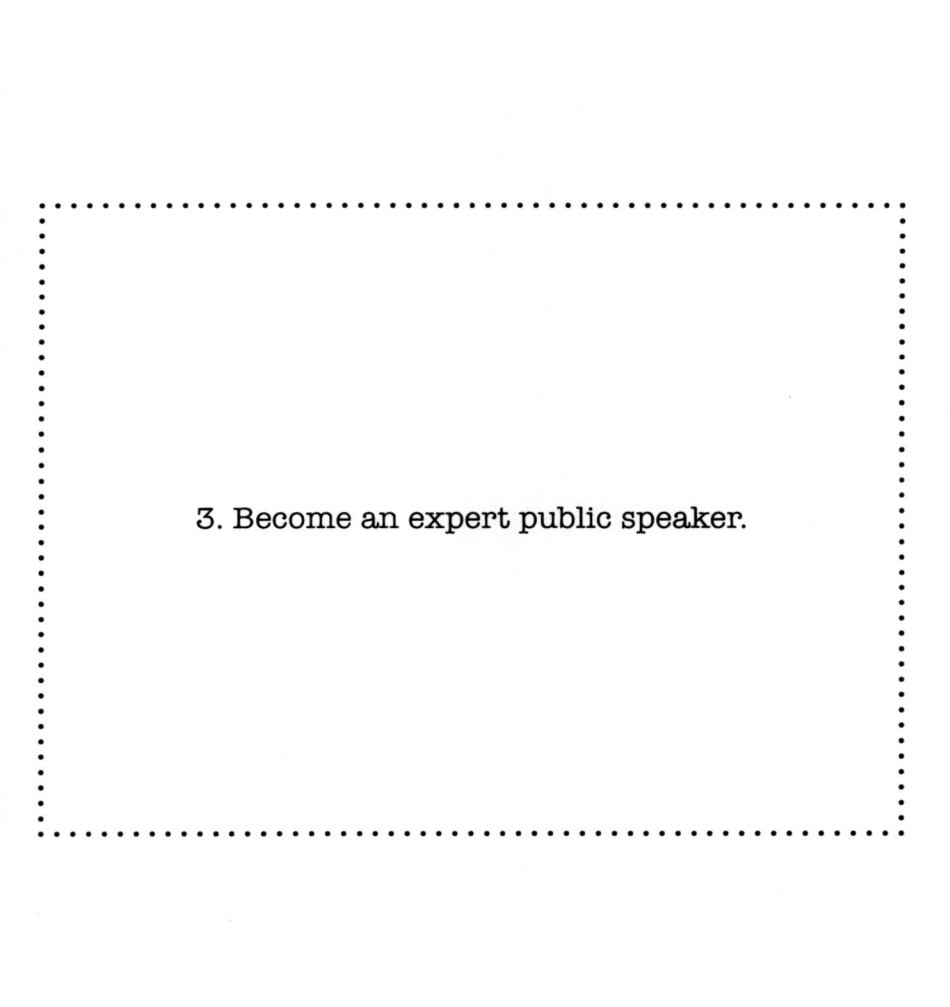

4. Write thank-you notes.

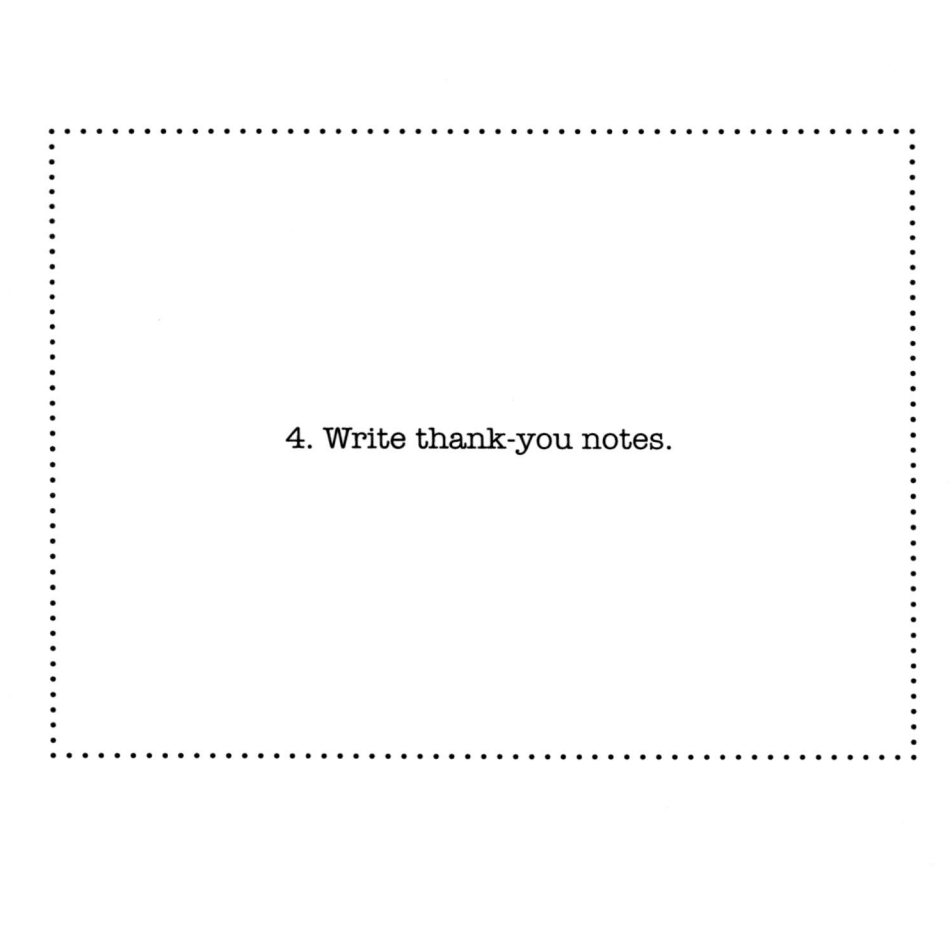

5. Appreciate your opportunities.

Don't take them for granted.

6. Use non-verbal communication.

7. Strive for excellence.

You can fool other people, but
you can't fool yourself.

8. Dress for success.

9. Develop a firm handshake.

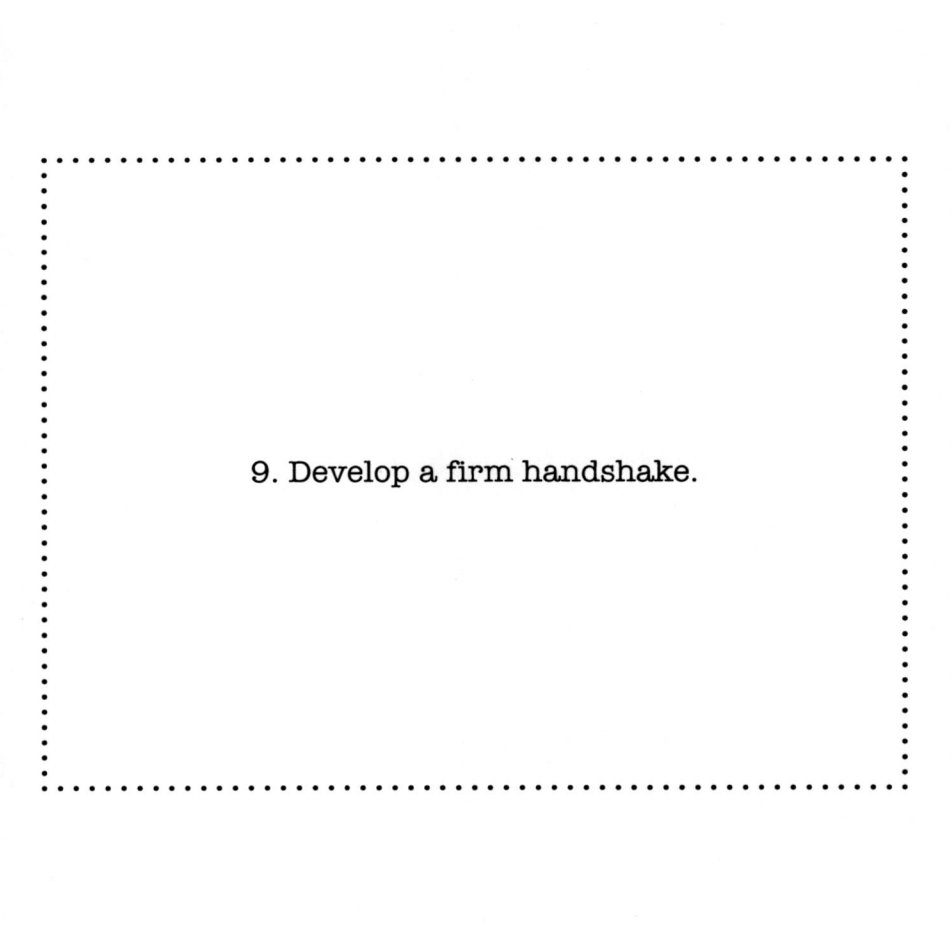

10. Remember people's names.

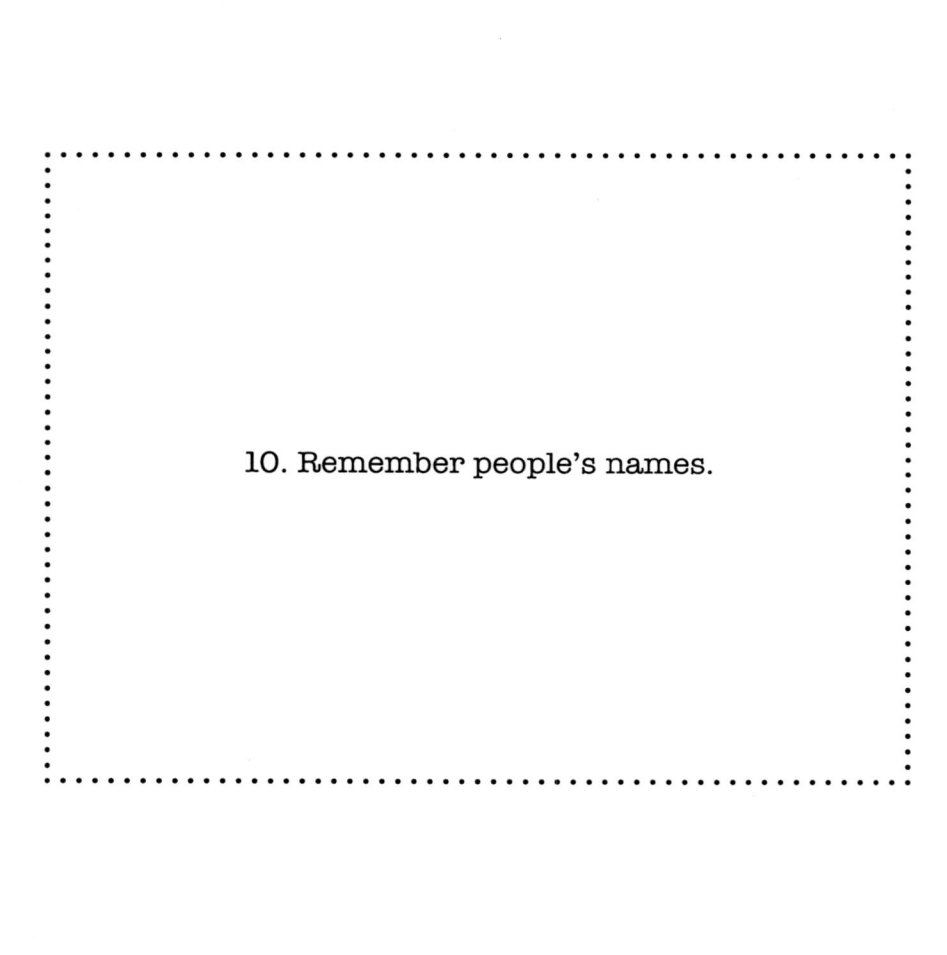

11. Listen instead of talk.

God gave you two ears and one mouth.
Use them in that proportion.

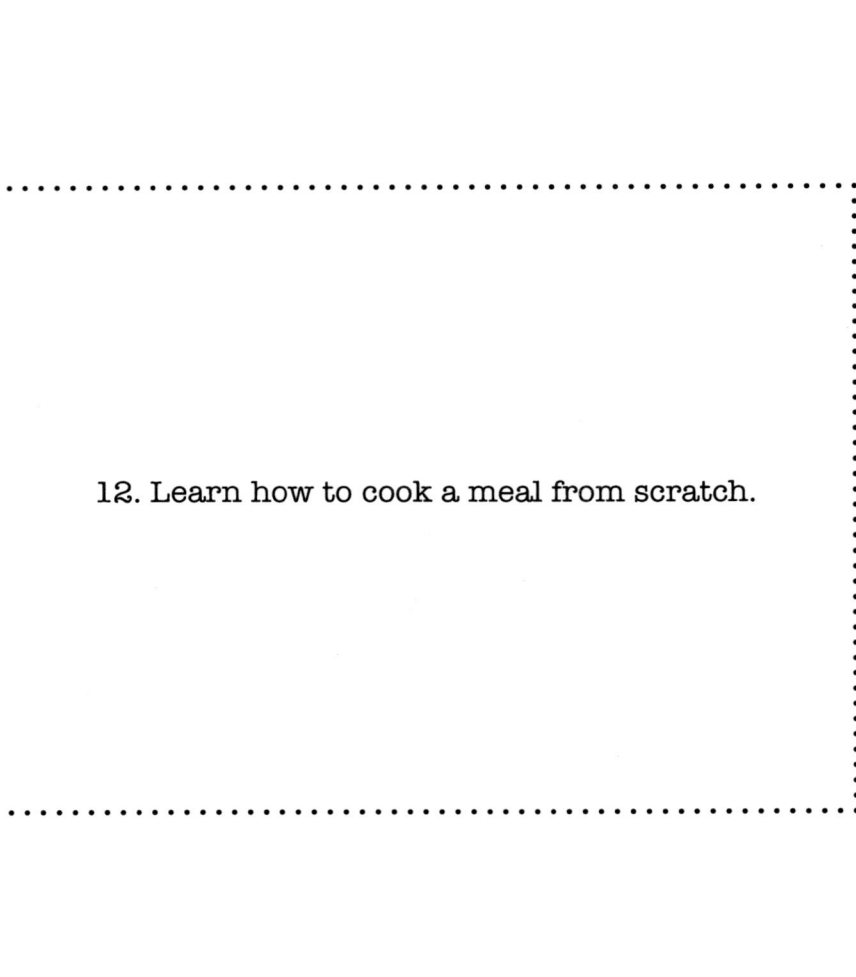

12. Learn how to cook a meal from scratch.

13. Ask questions of elders.

14. Admit your mistakes.

15. Take risks to become something great.

A boat safe in the harbor rots.

16. Eat well.

You are what you eat.

17. Work out.

18. Read every day.

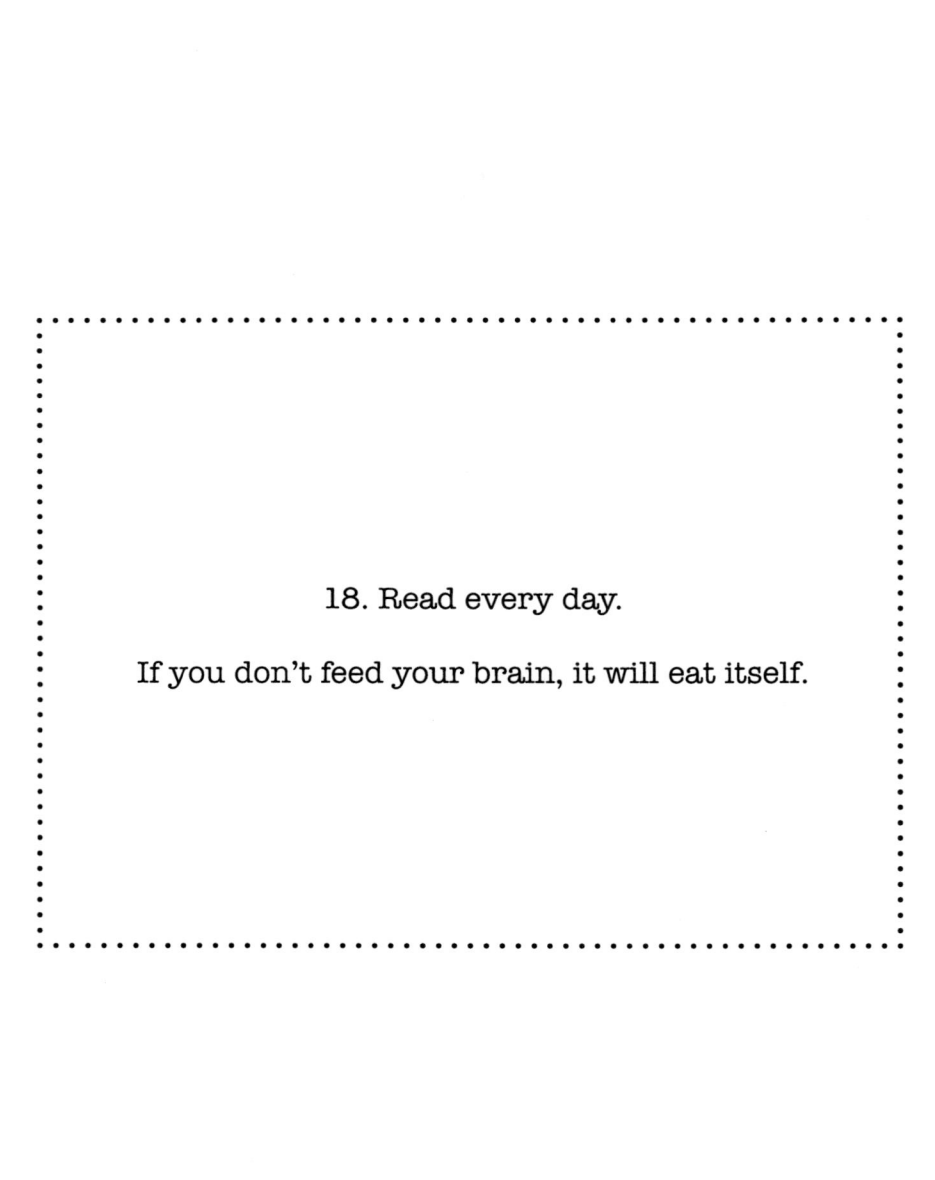

If you don't feed your brain, it will eat itself.

19. Do something fun every day.

20. Learn clean jokes.

21. Wherever you are, be there.

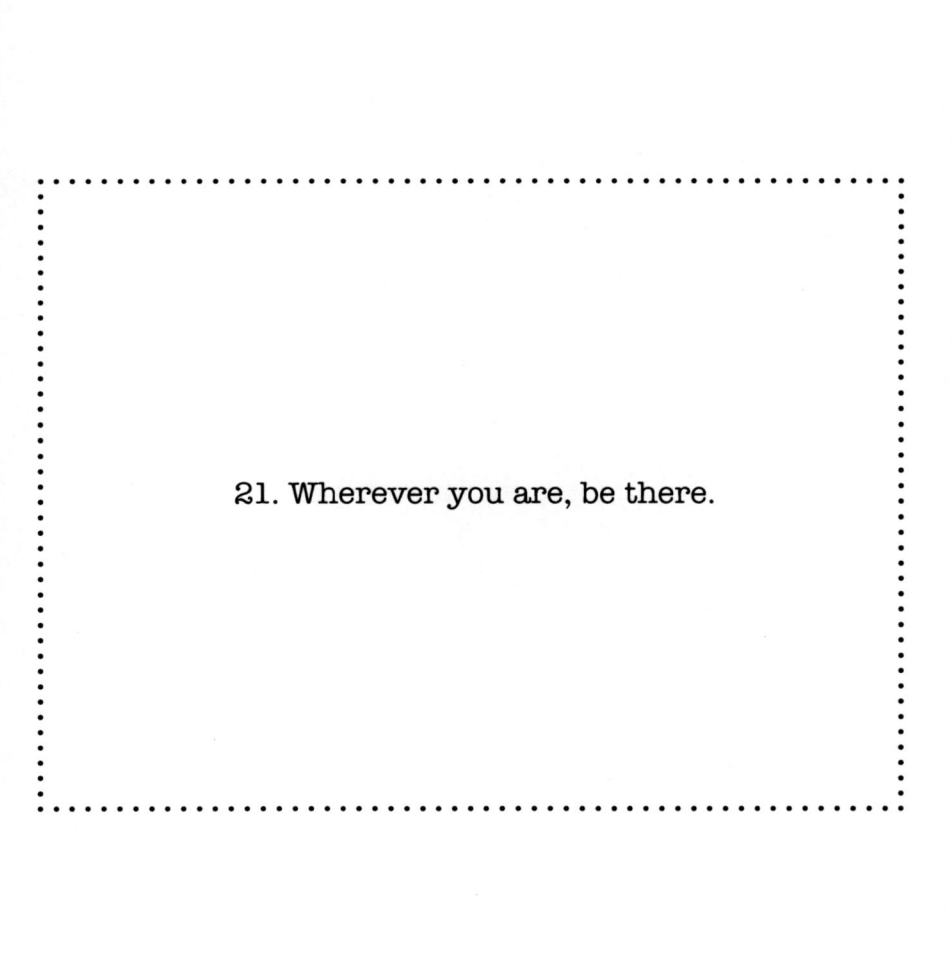

22. Hang out with your parents on a Saturday night.

23. Teach a class.

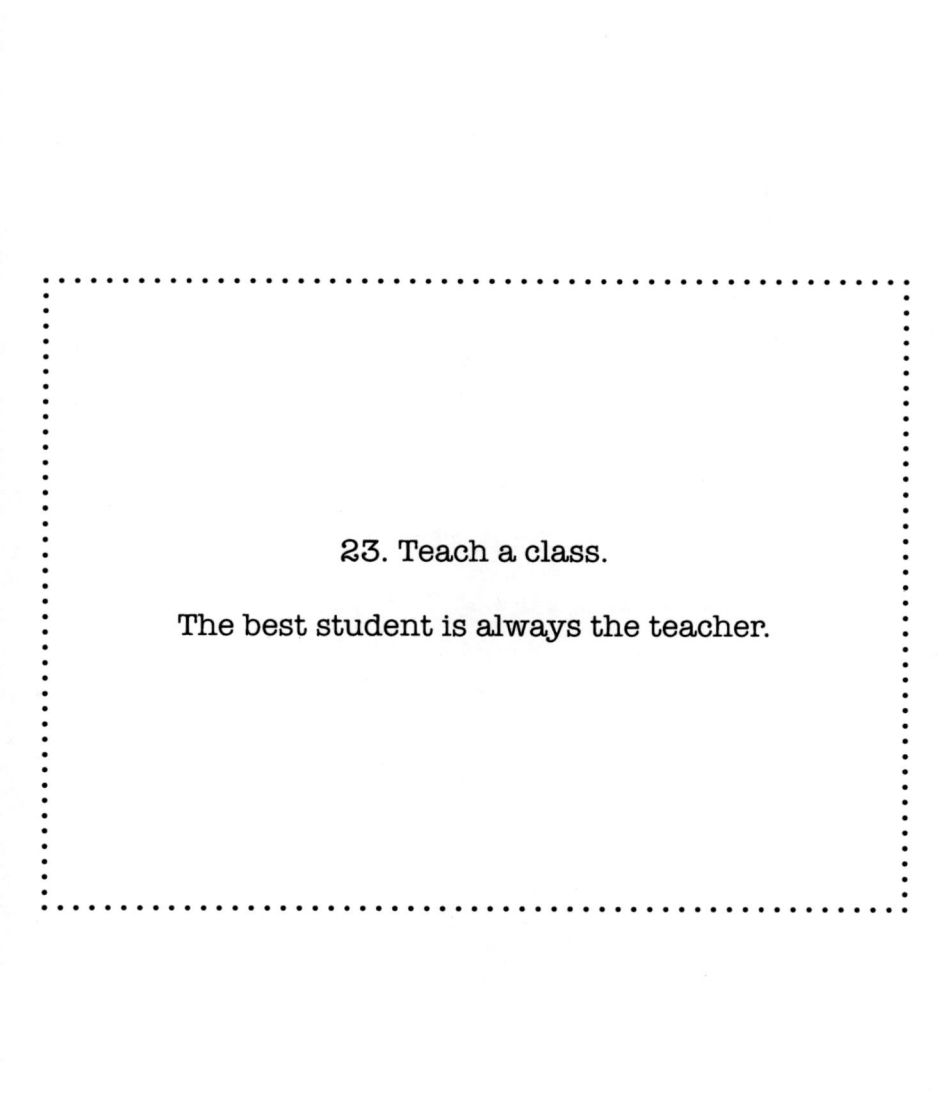

The best student is always the teacher.

24. Have a hobby that you love.

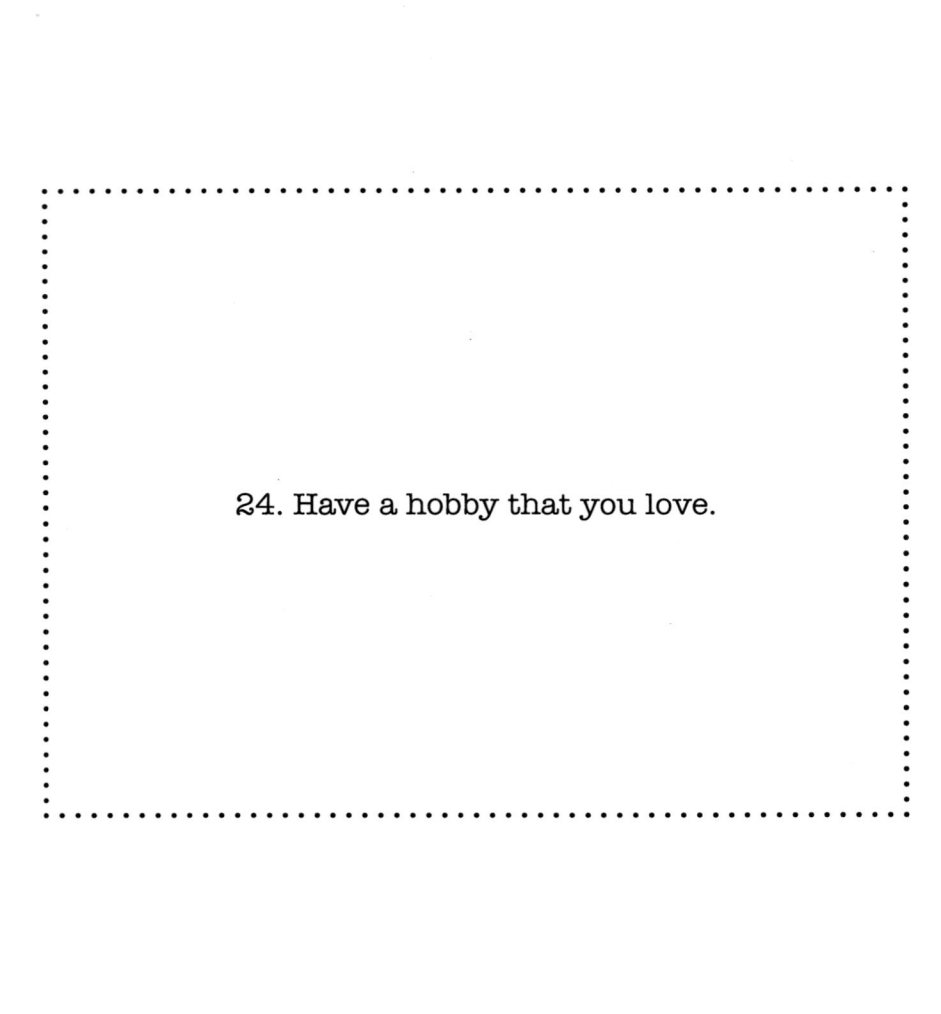

25. Call your grandparents once a week.

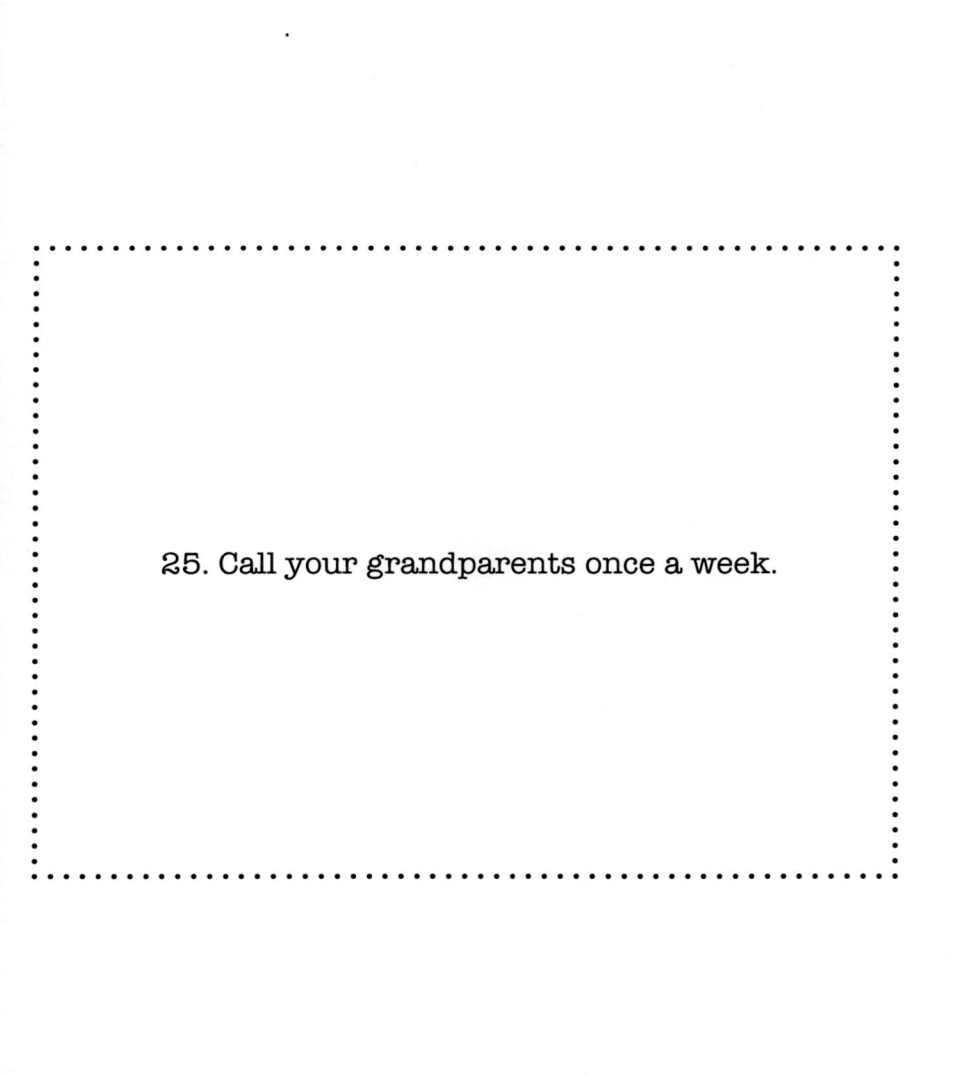

26. Stop asking why and start asking how.

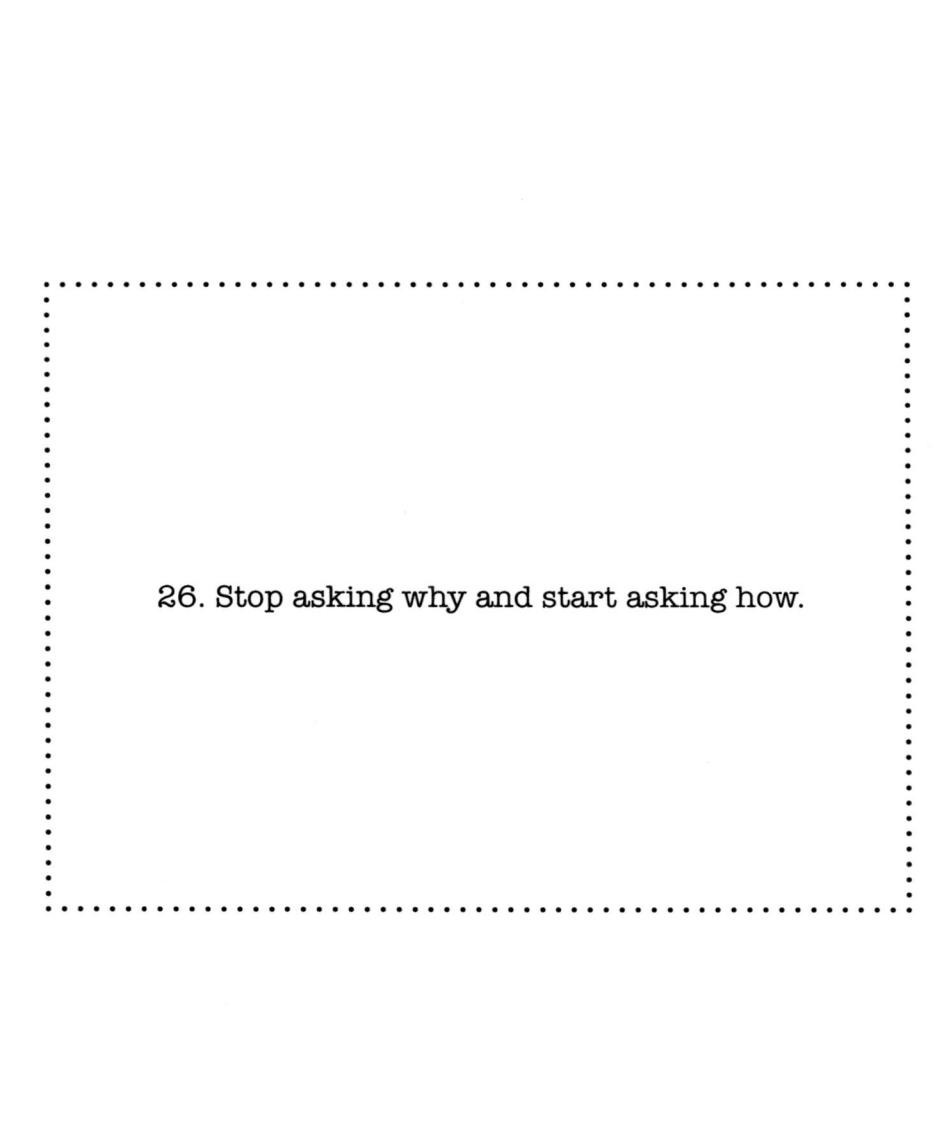

27. Become spiritual.

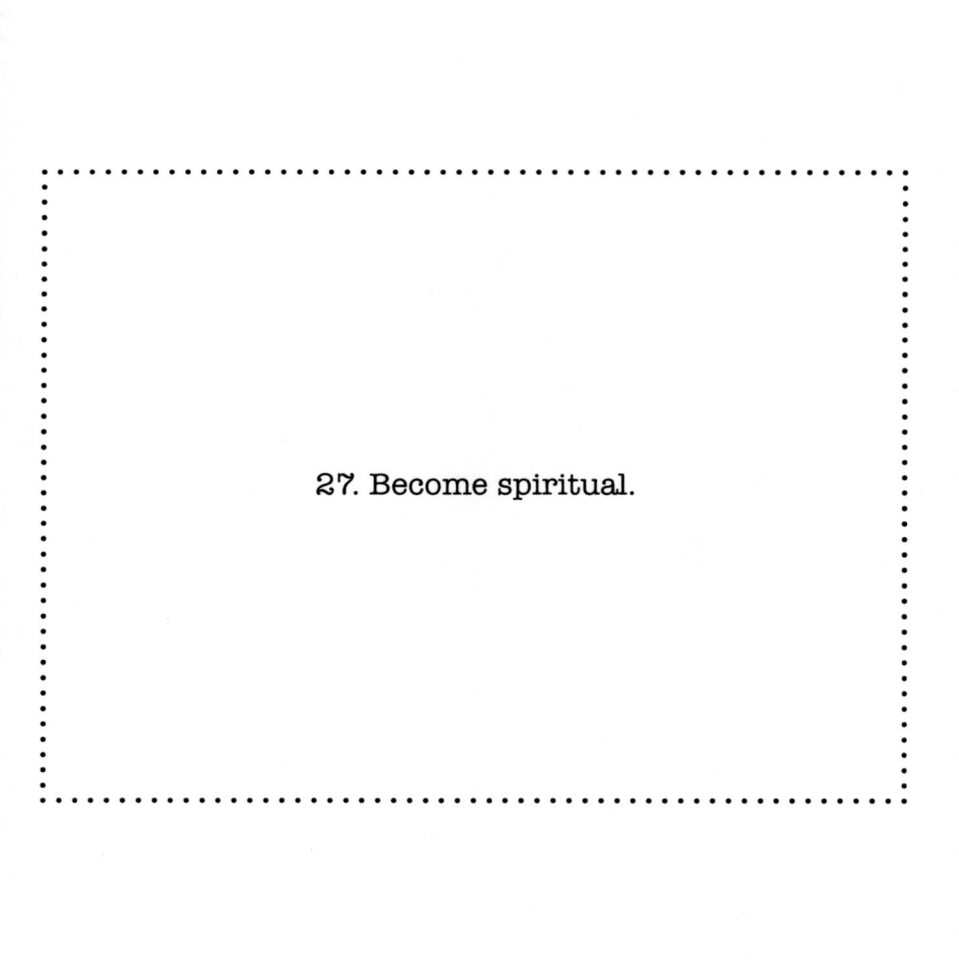

28. Do your research before forming an opinion.

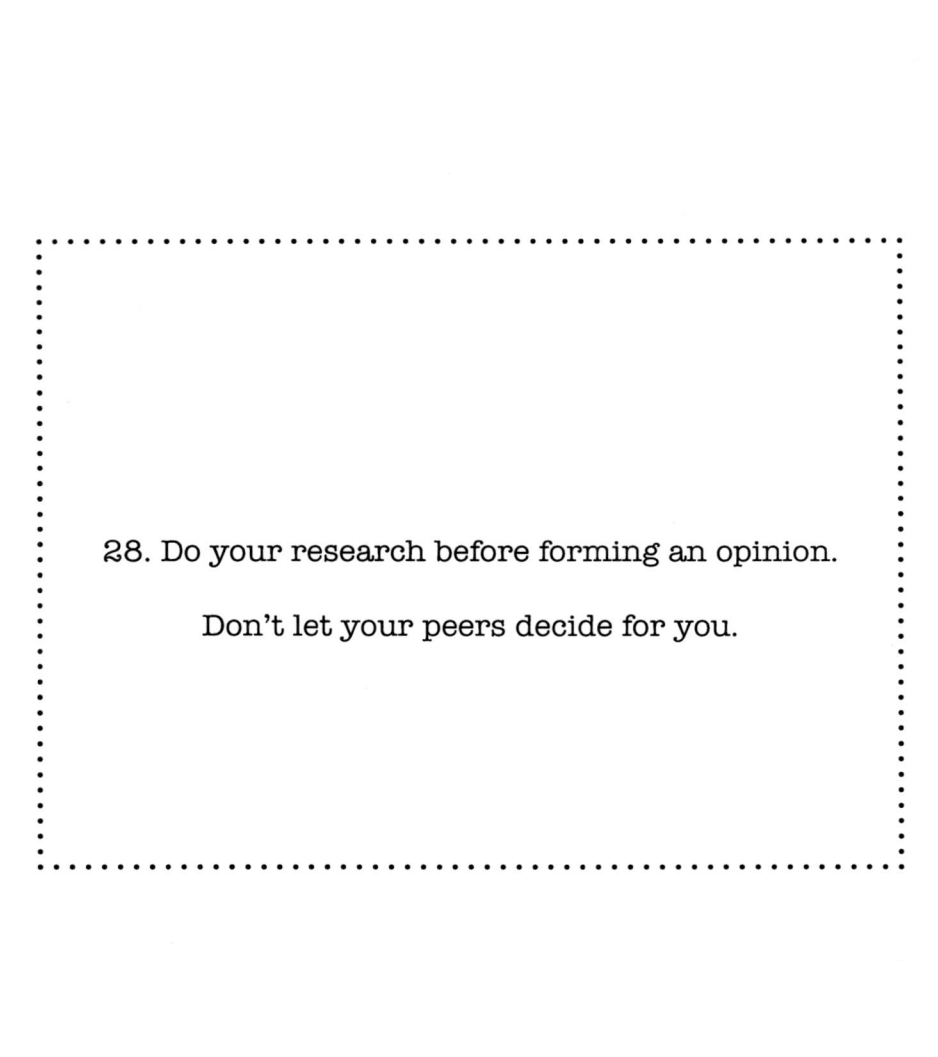

Don't let your peers decide for you.

29. Be strong with your convictions.

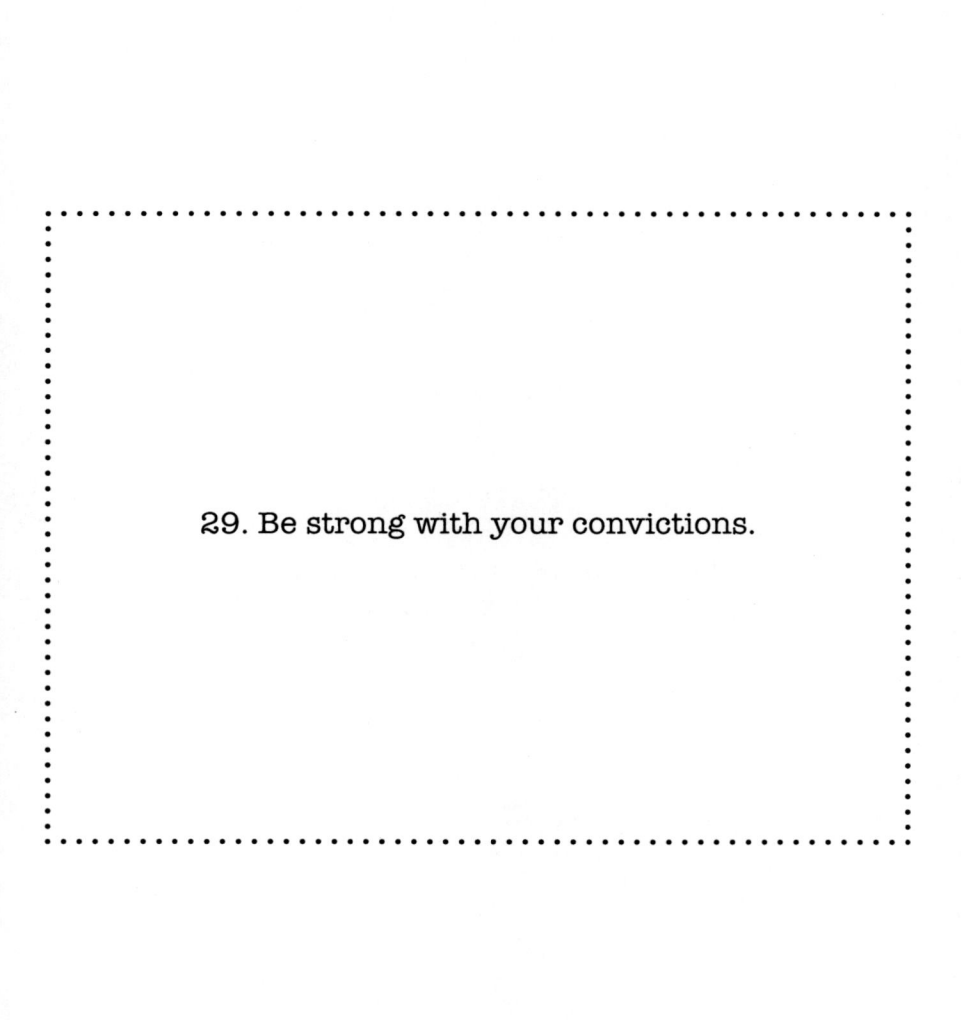

30. Don't lie.

You'll never have to worry about what you said if you always tell the truth.

31. Don't get into debt.

Save your money.

32. Manage your checkbook.

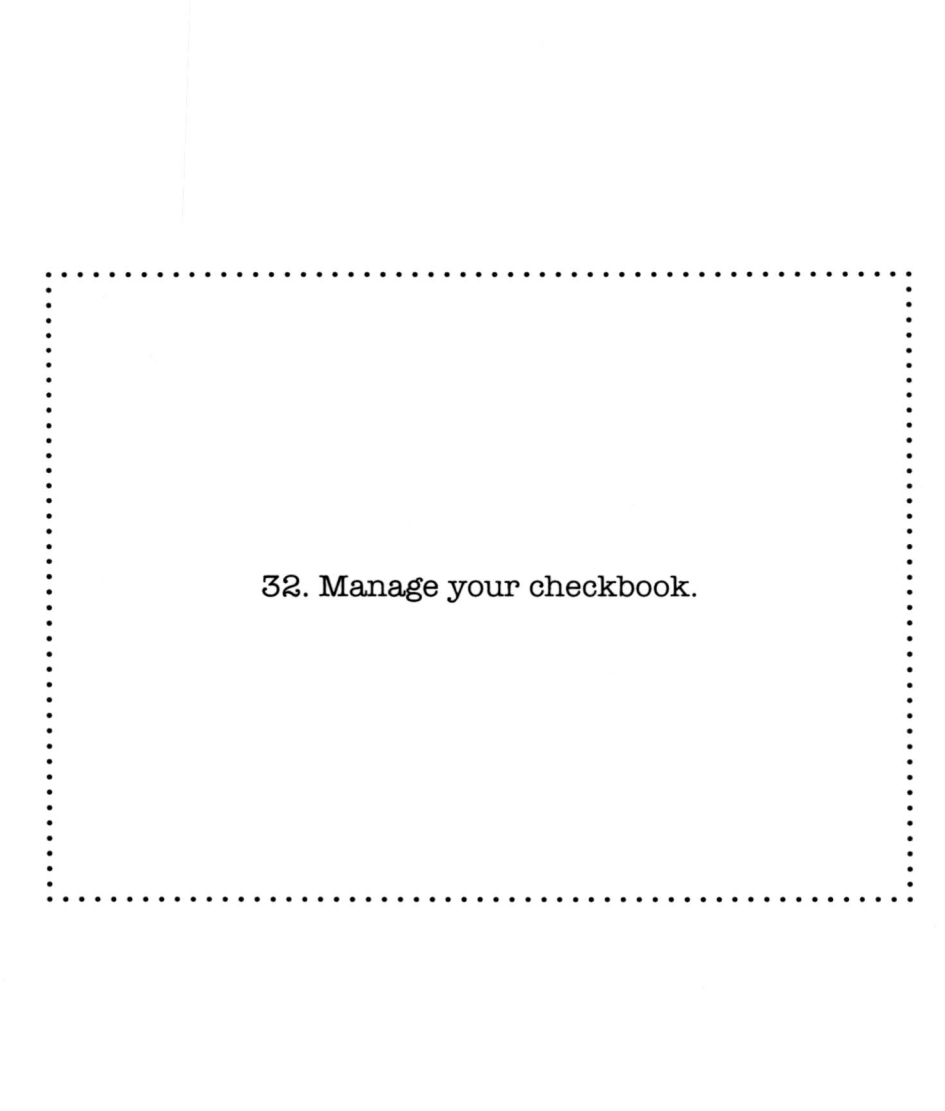

33. Head a committee.

34. Go to a town meeting.

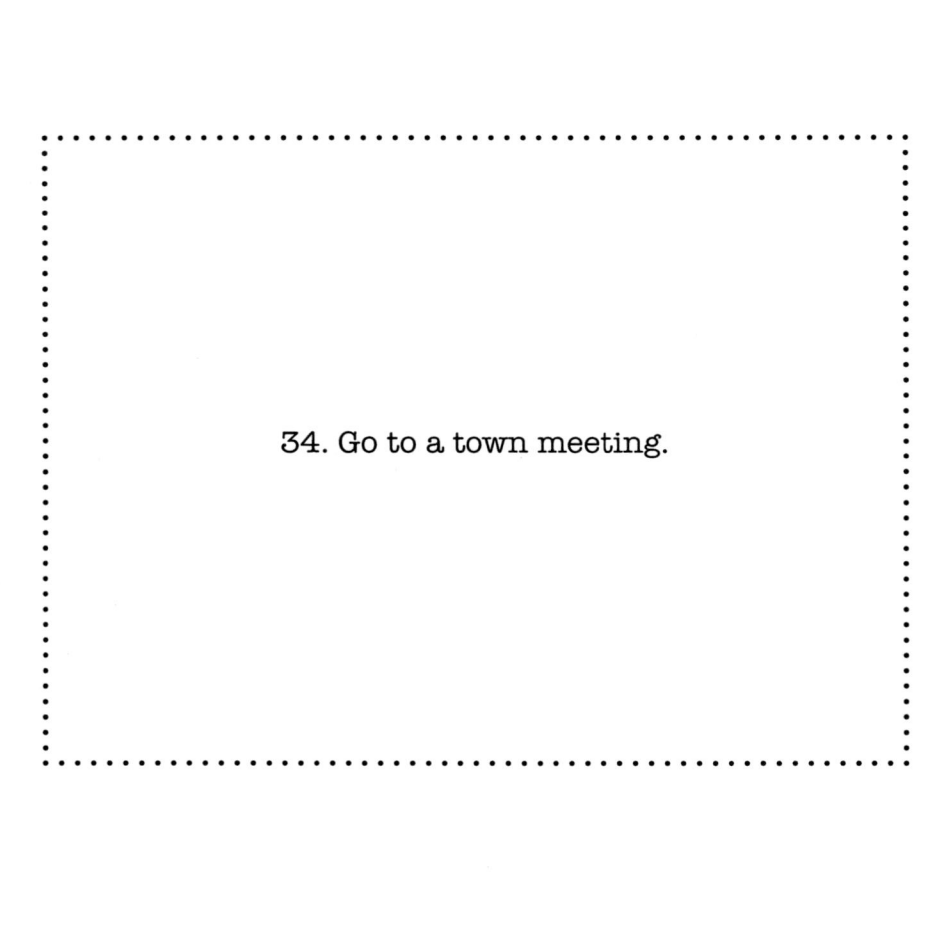

35. Write an editorial for your local newspaper.

36. Do something nice anonymously.

37. Learn about other cultures.

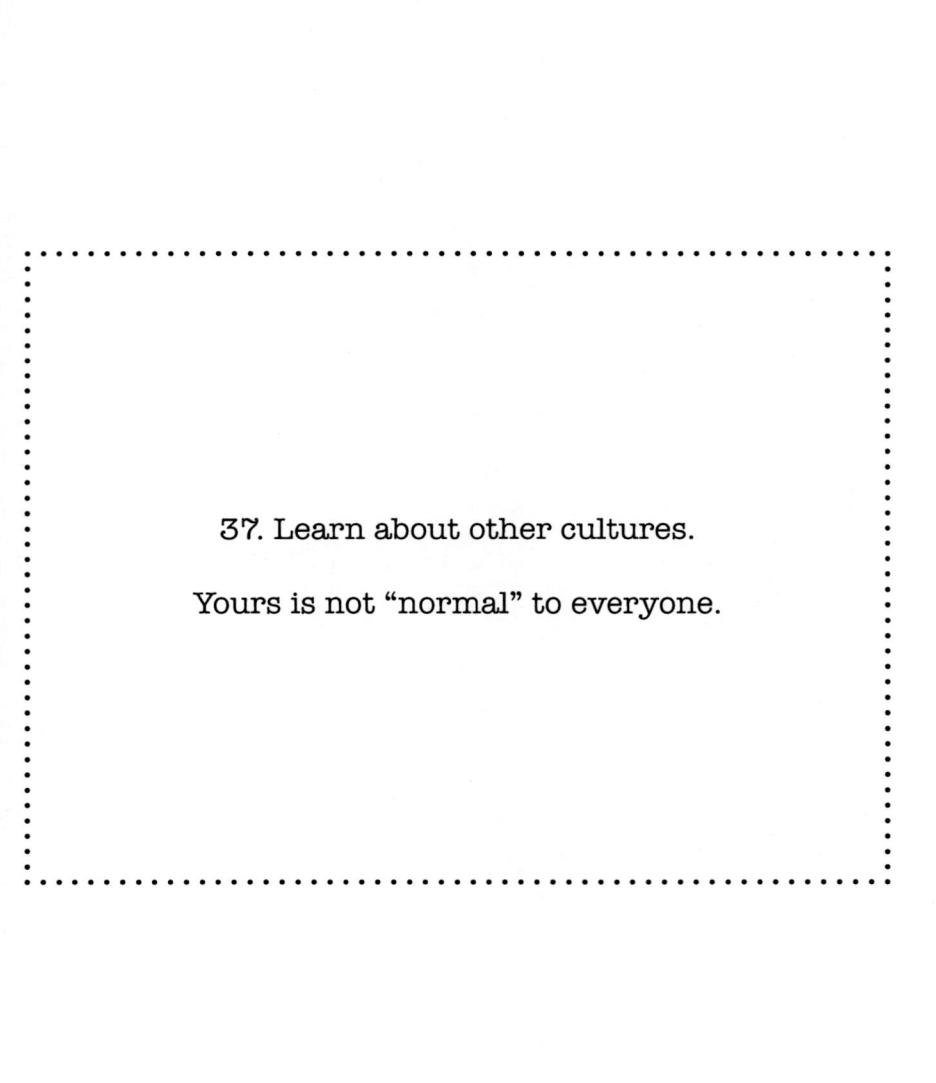

Yours is not "normal" to everyone.

38. Use the KISS technique: Keep It Simple, Silly.

39. Help your younger brothers, sisters or cousins with their homework.

40. Start to worry when you are acting exactly like everyone else.

41. Get involved in something in which you have no natural talent.

42. Get a part-time job to save money for college.

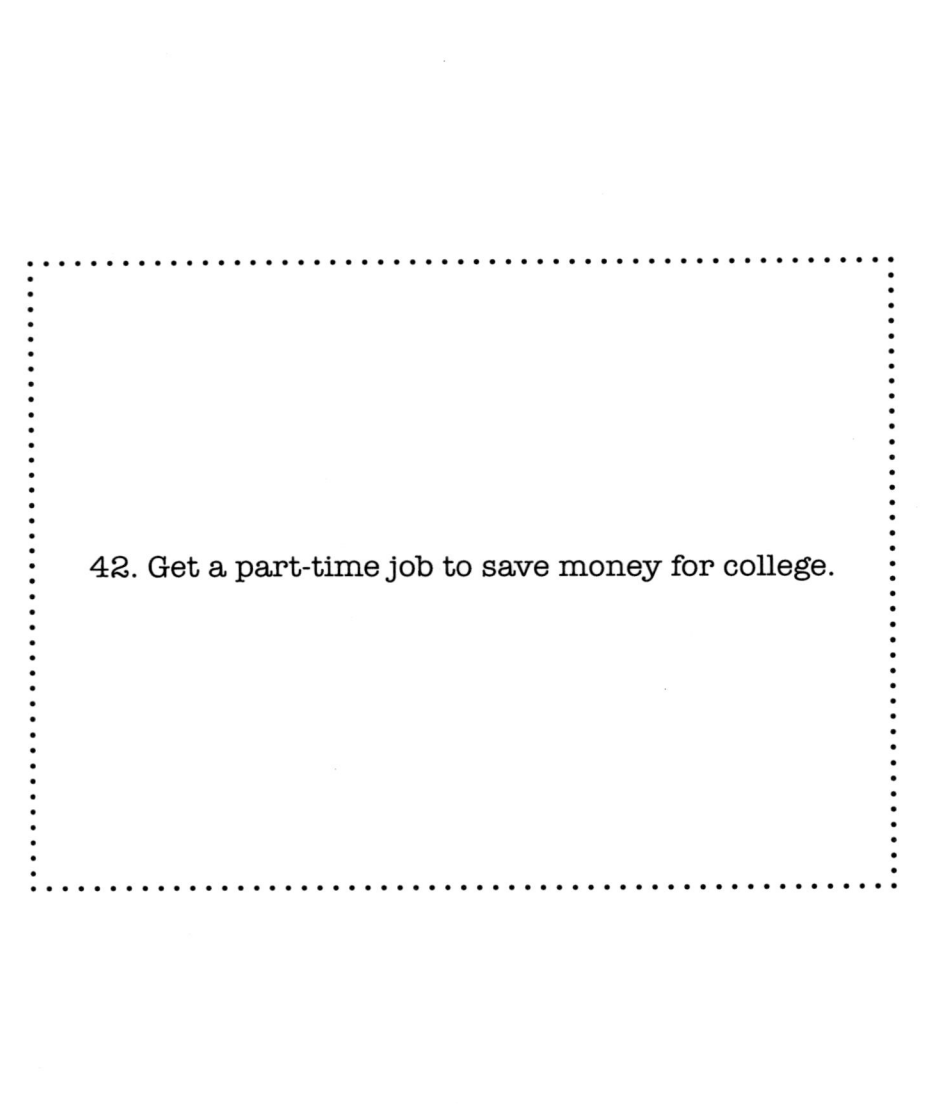

43. Spend one hour a night away from the TV
and away from the Internet.

Instead, talk with your family,
go for a walk or read.

44. Take a course in something that has nothing to do with your career goals, such as European history, Greek philosophy or Mandarin Chinese.

45. Become fluent in another language.

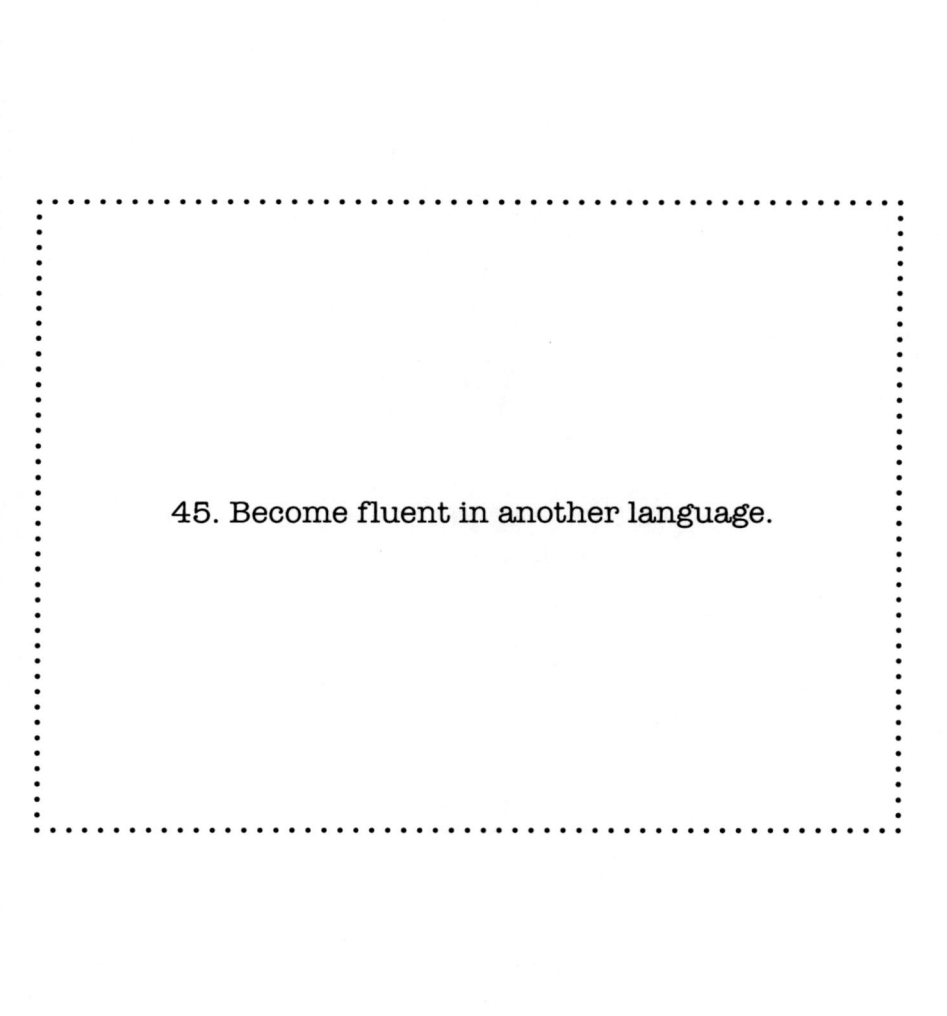

46. Sit in the front of the classroom, and raise your hand often.

47. Start a club.

48. Say goodbye to friends
that can't help you grow.

49. Set goals.

50. Make lists of things to do, and cross off items as you finish them.

Don't start number two on the list until you have finished number one.

51. See who you want to be in the future, and work backwards.

52. Simplify your life.

If you are doing anything today that you wish you never started, get rid of it.

53. Take a long walk by yourself every now and then.

54. Find something good in everyone.

Everybody is your superior in some way.

55. Learn how your country's economy works.

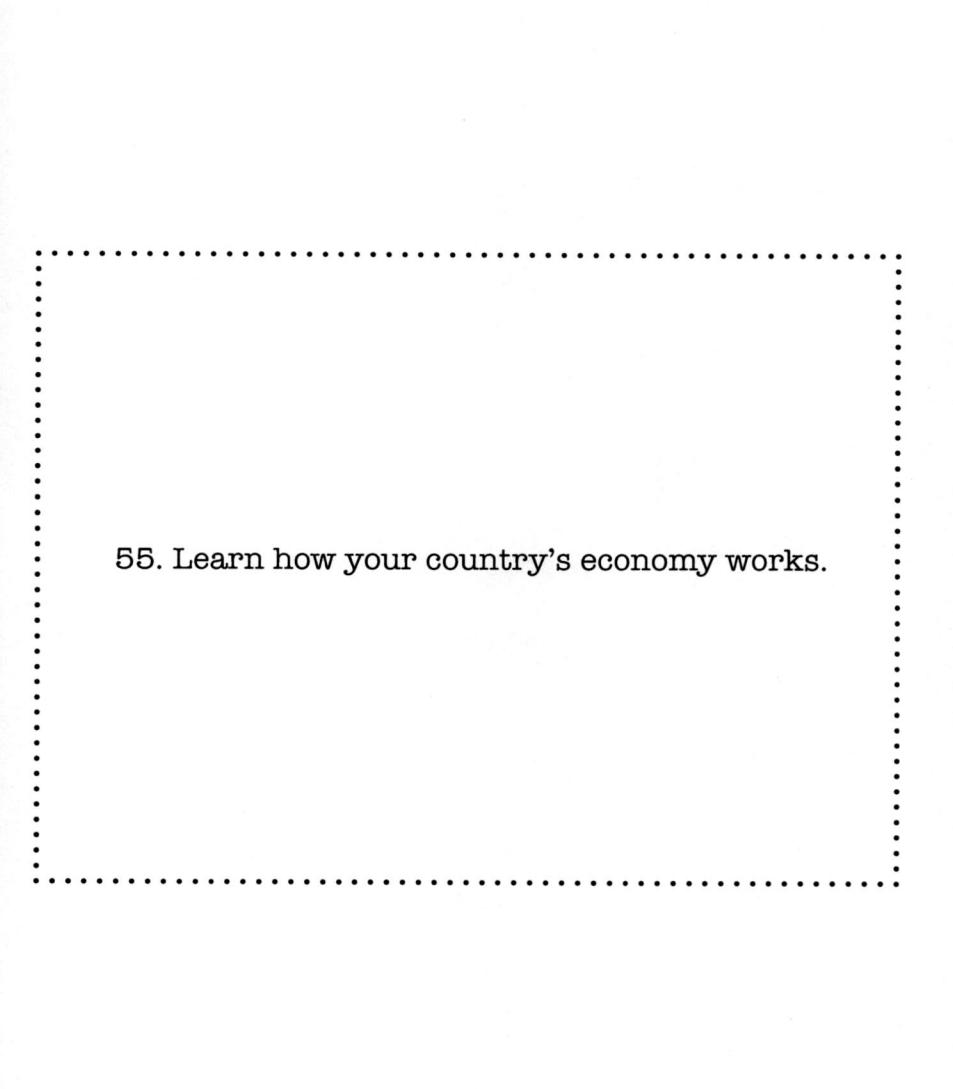

56. Have respect for every job.

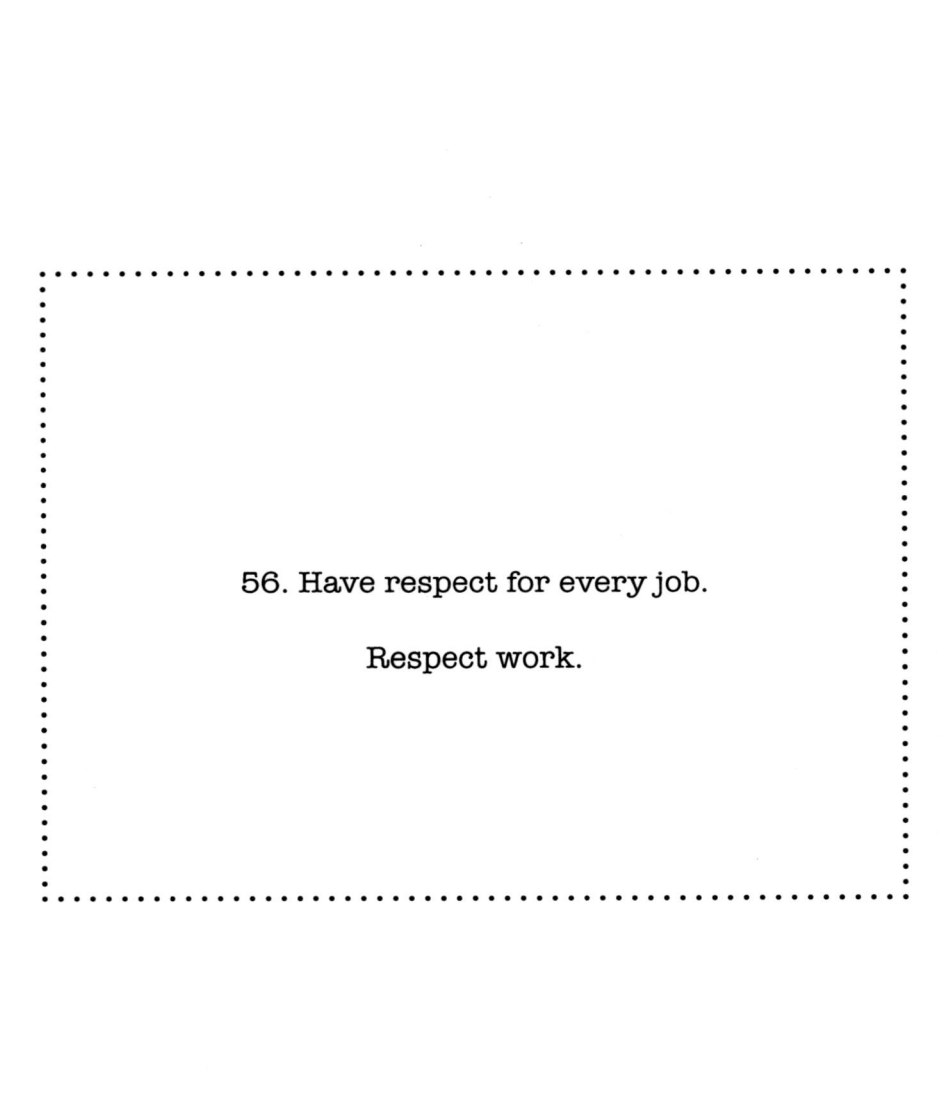

Respect work.

57. Listen to your parents, but don't let them tell you who you are going to be.

58. Wear shoes, not sneakers,
to your place of worship.

59. Get an internship.

60. Plan your legacy now.

61. Give to charity.

62. Learn how to change a tire.

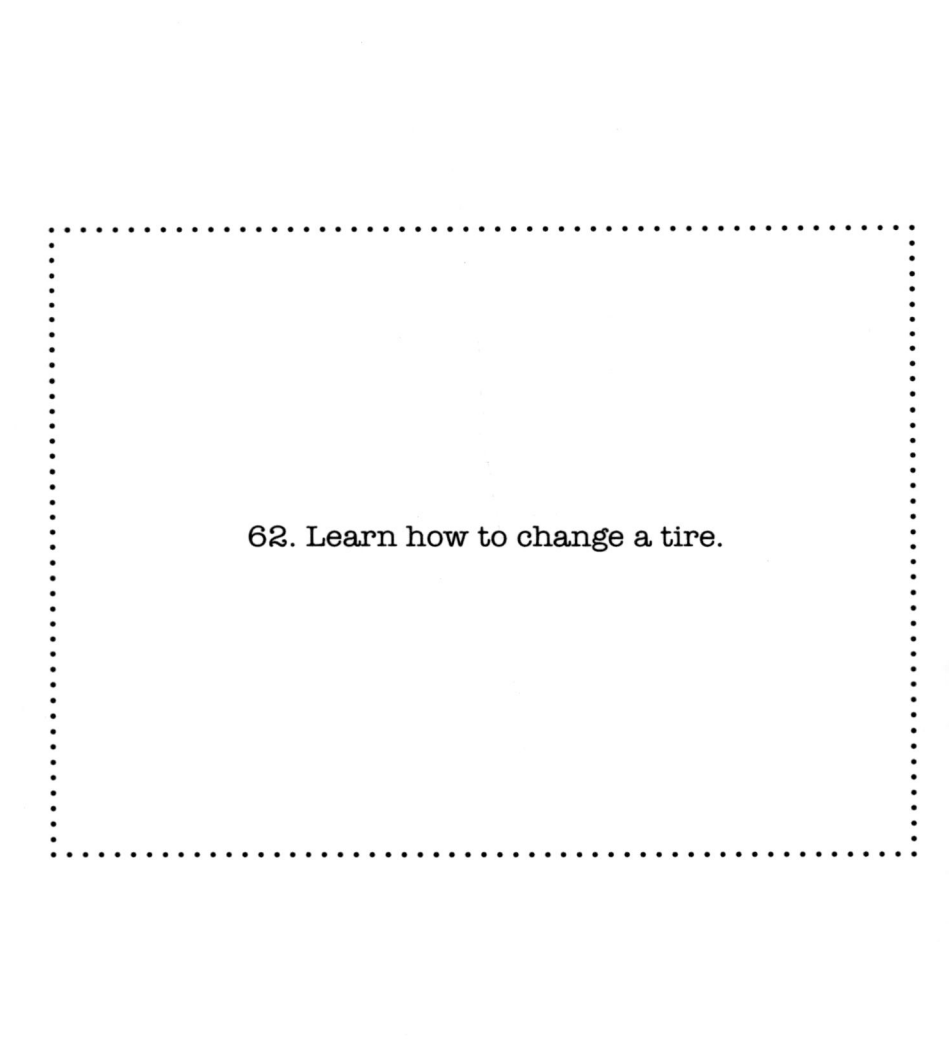

63. Learn how to barbeque well.

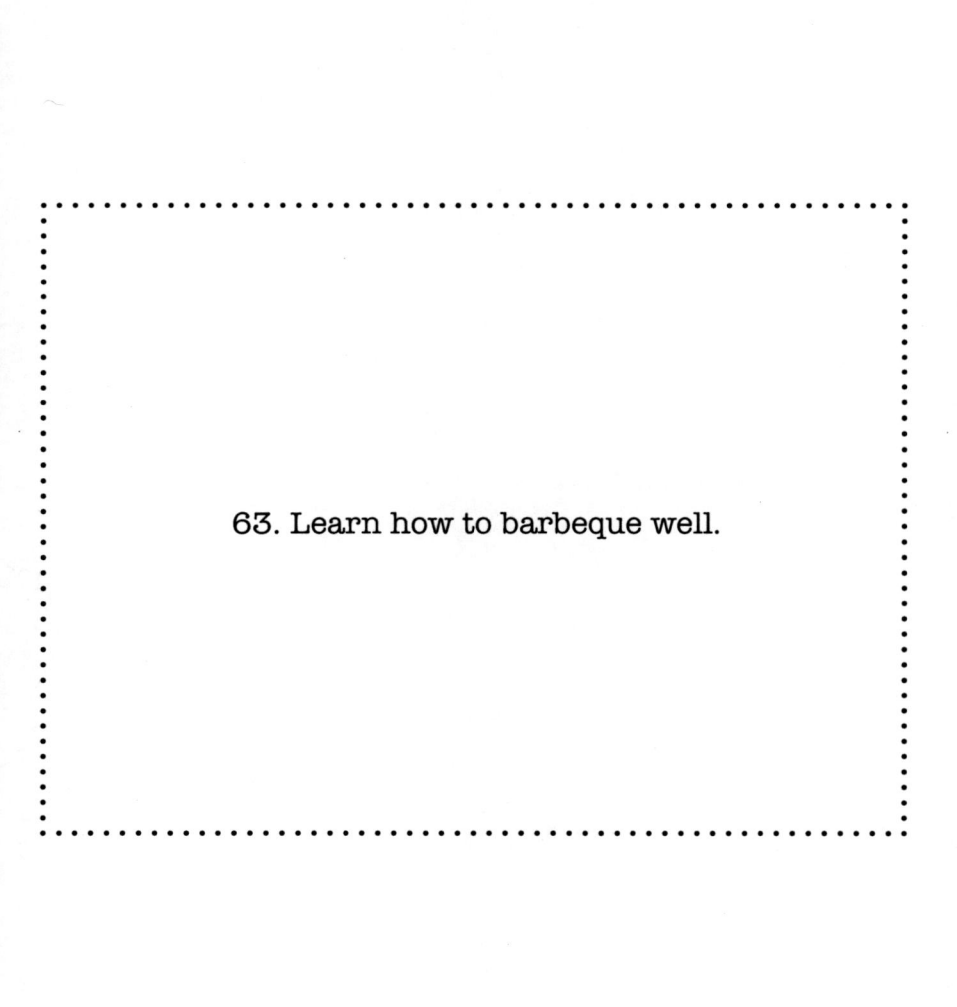

64. Take good care of your possessions.

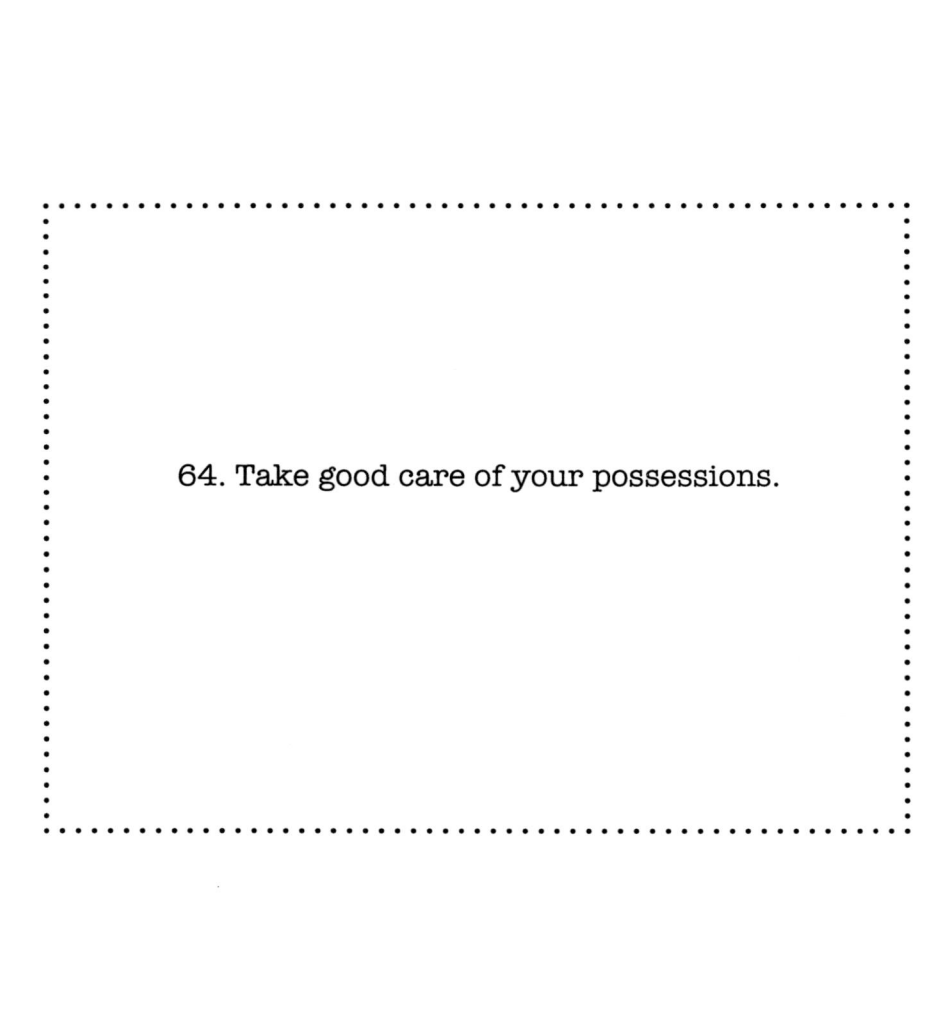

65. Learn about past wars, and gain an appreciation of what sacrifices were made so that you can enjoy the freedom you have.

66. Learn about your heritage so you can appreciate what your ancestors went through to give you what you have today.

67. Don't be a victim.

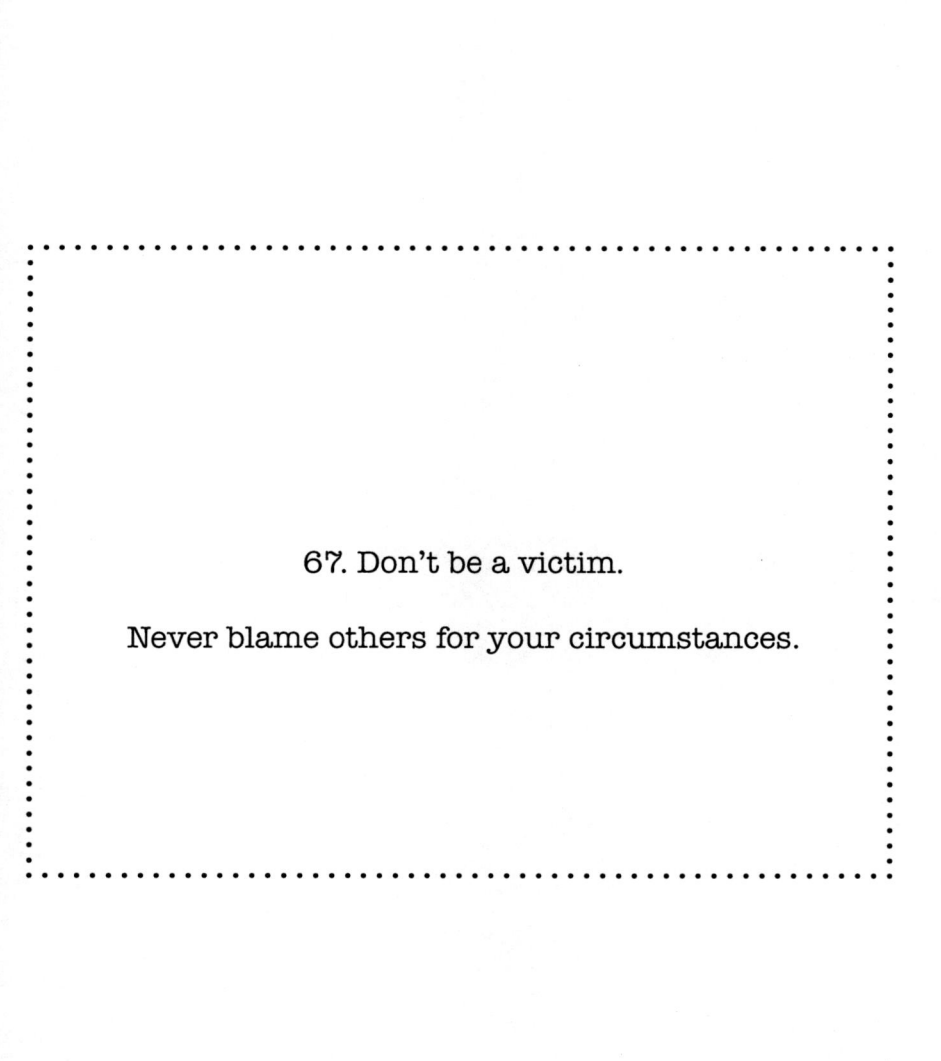

Never blame others for your circumstances.

68. Don't let anyone ever tell you that you can't do something.

69. Don't worry
about things that
you can't control.

70. Don't think too much about
the meaning of life.

Get so involved in the fabric of life that
you don't even stop to think about
the meaning of it.

71. Don't let popular music, movies and TV
influence your personality.

They'll be gone in three years;
your personality won't.

72. Work on making your insides more attractive than your outside.

As Judge Judy says, "Beauty fades, stupid is forever."

73. Practice saying no.

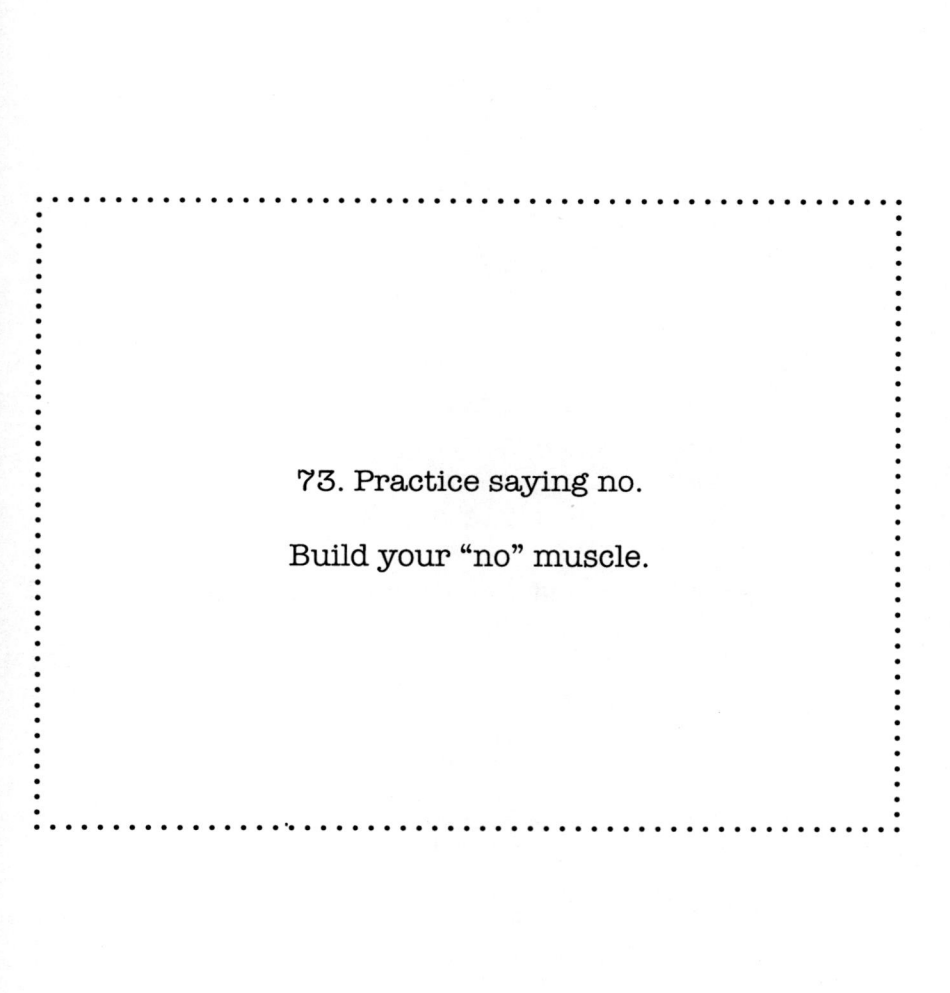

Build your "no" muscle.

74. Acknowledge that your parents have been around a lot longer than you, are probably smarter than you, and ultimately have your best interests at heart.

They are not just having fun torturing you.

75. Teach your grandparents how to text and use e-mail.

76. Get involved in the family business.

No, not the family pizzeria; the actual business of running a household.

Help out.

Ask to get involved.

Don't live in a bubble.

77. Plant a garden and take care of it.

78. Eat nutritiously every day.

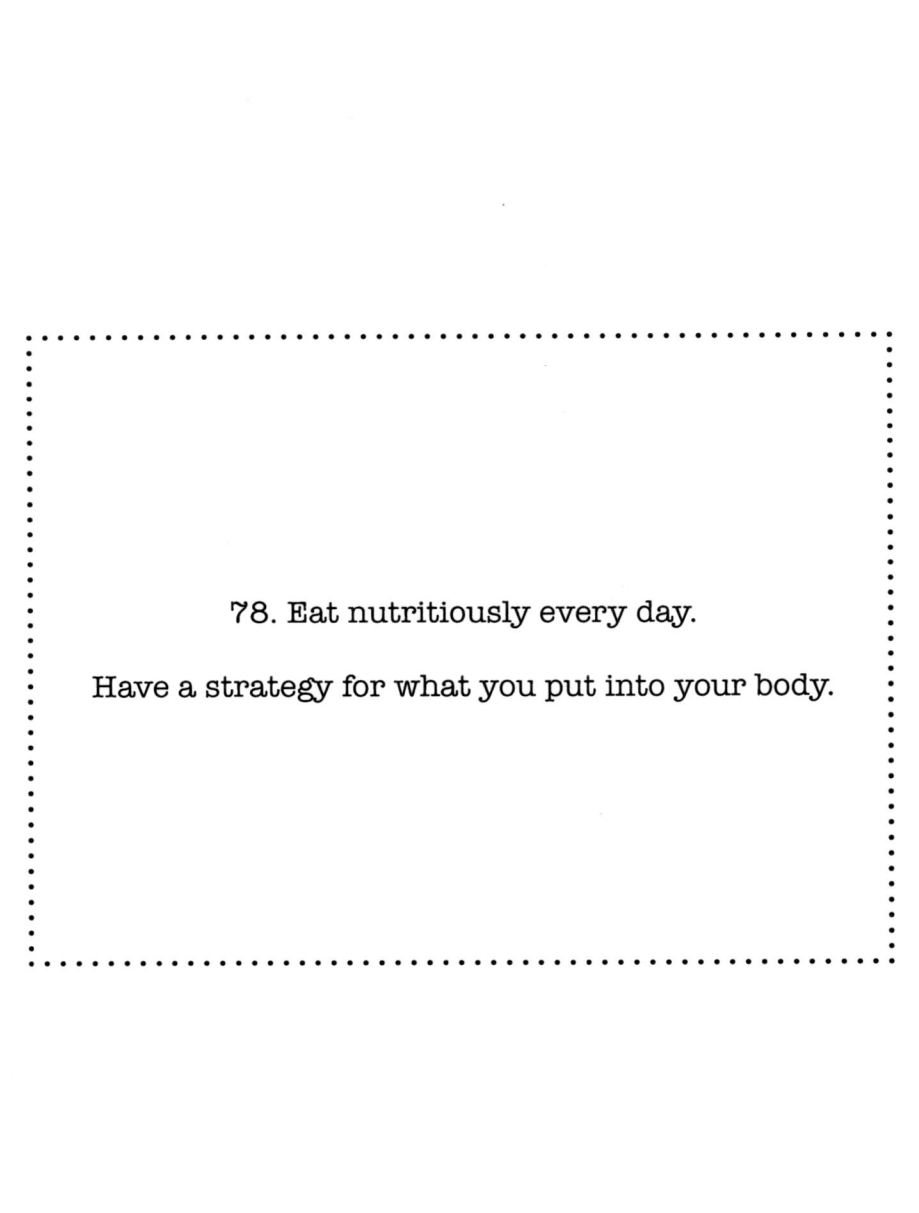

Have a strategy for what you put into your body.

79. Learn how to cook.

Have your own signature recipe for a breakfast, lunch and dinner meal.

80. Take a leadership course.

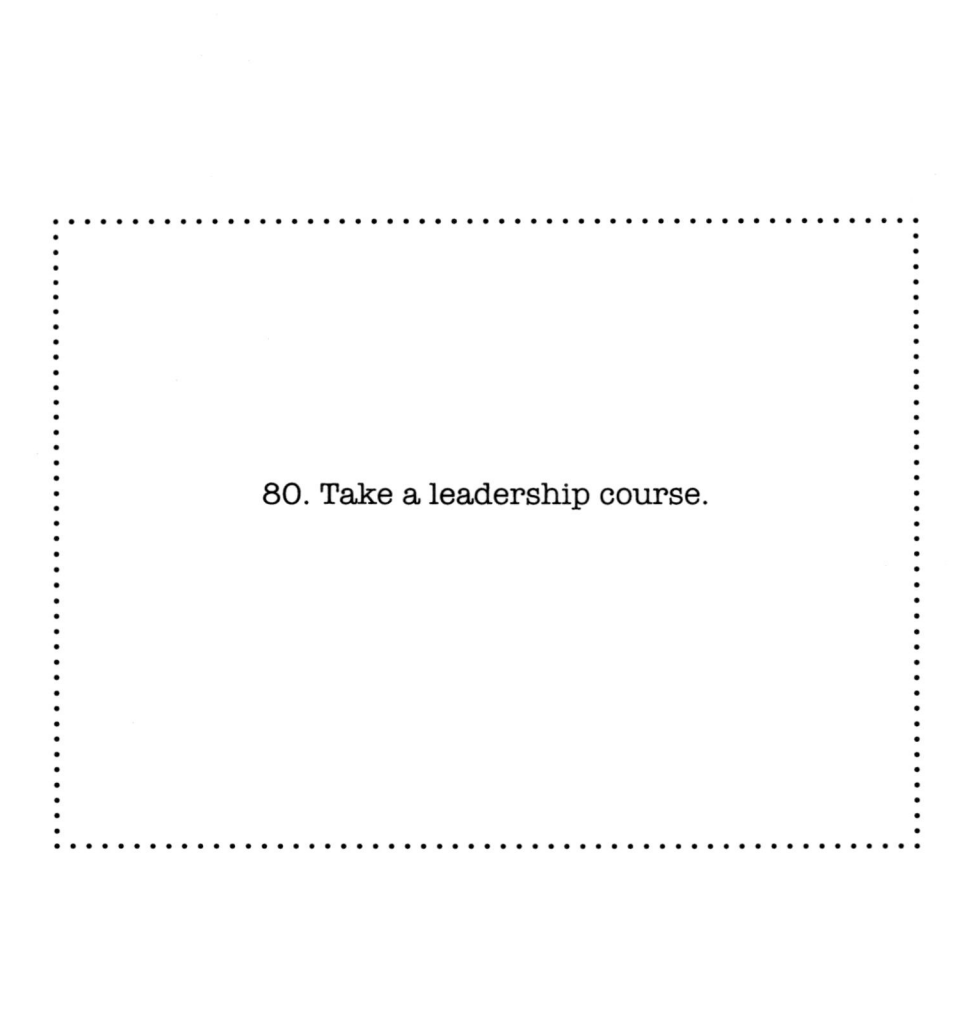

81. Read at least one book a month.

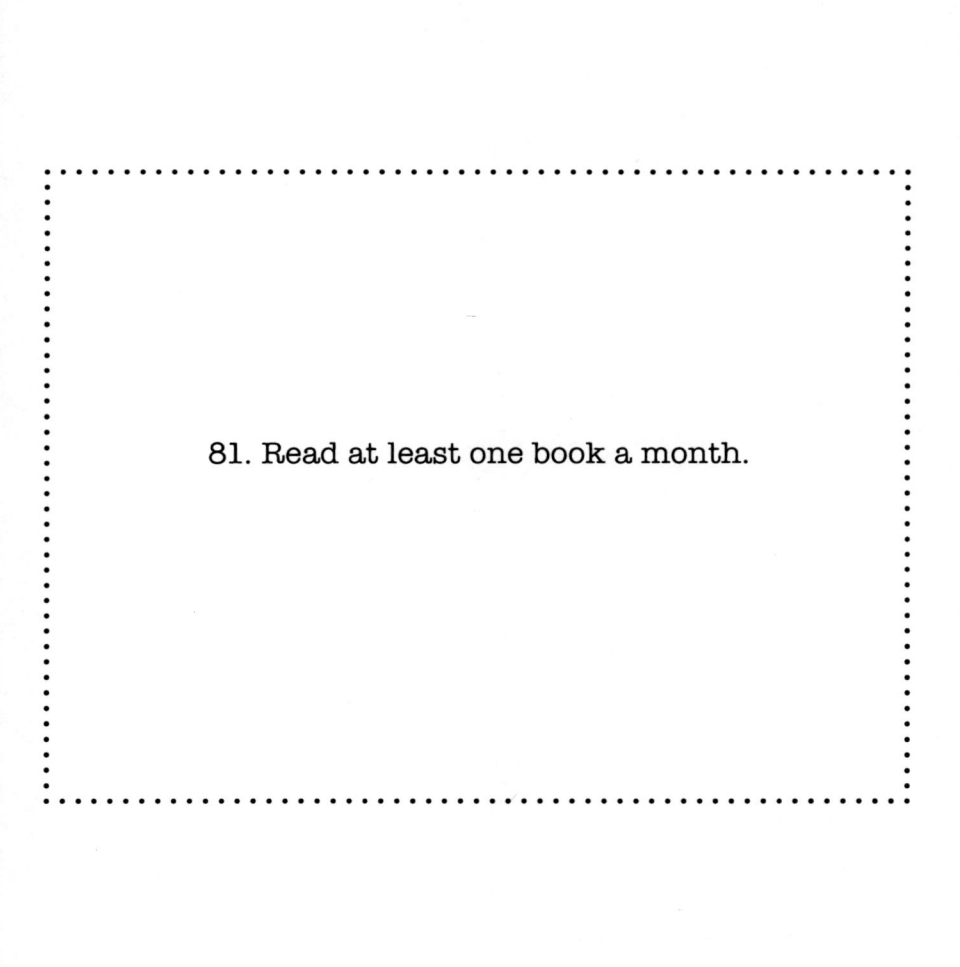

82. Have pride.

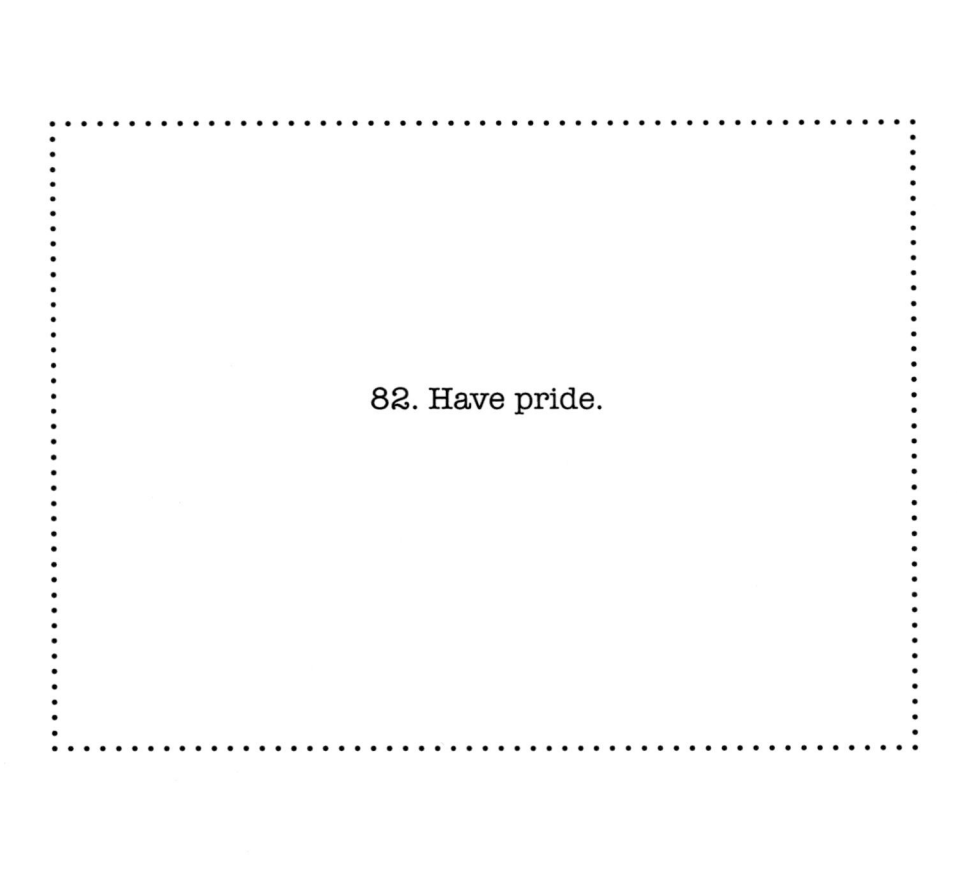

83. When in doubt about doing something questionable, ask yourself this question: Would my parents be proud of me?

84. Volunteer to help the elderly.

85. Volunteer to work with sick children.

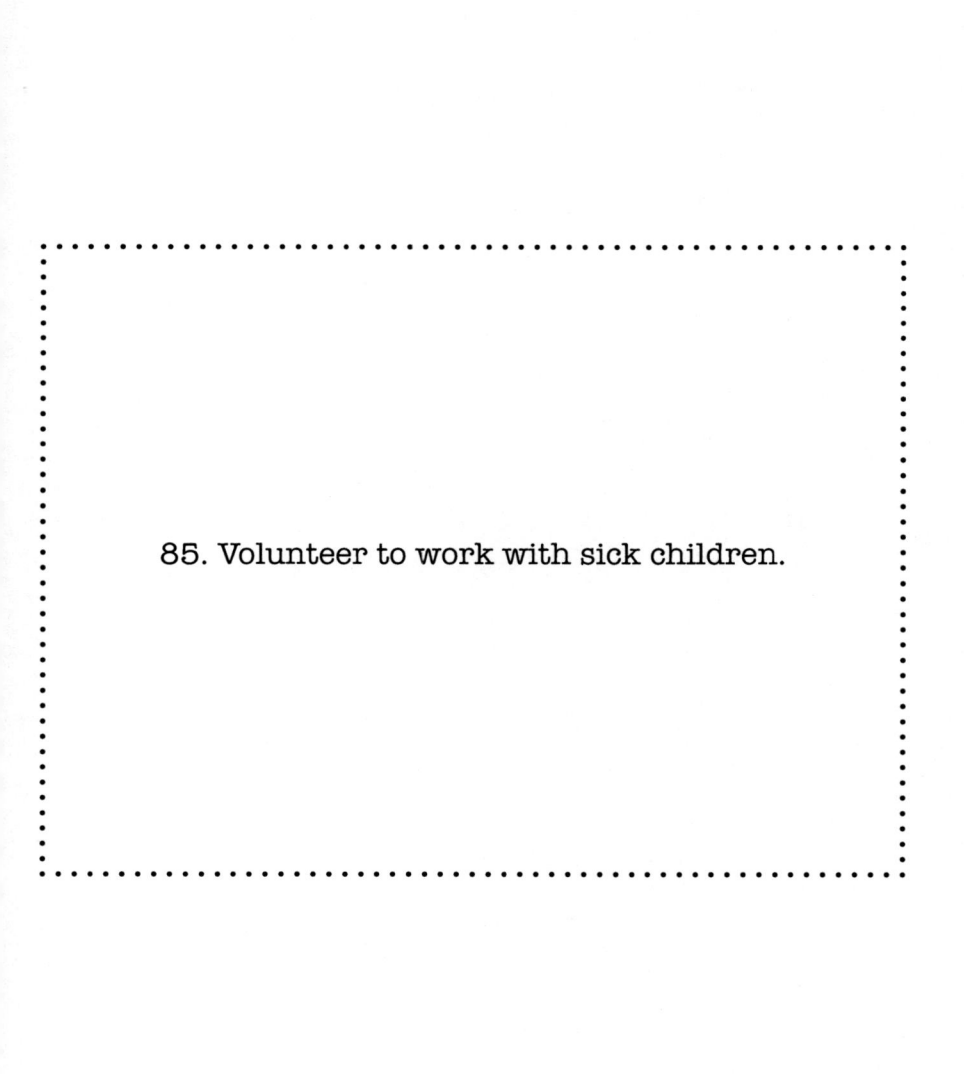

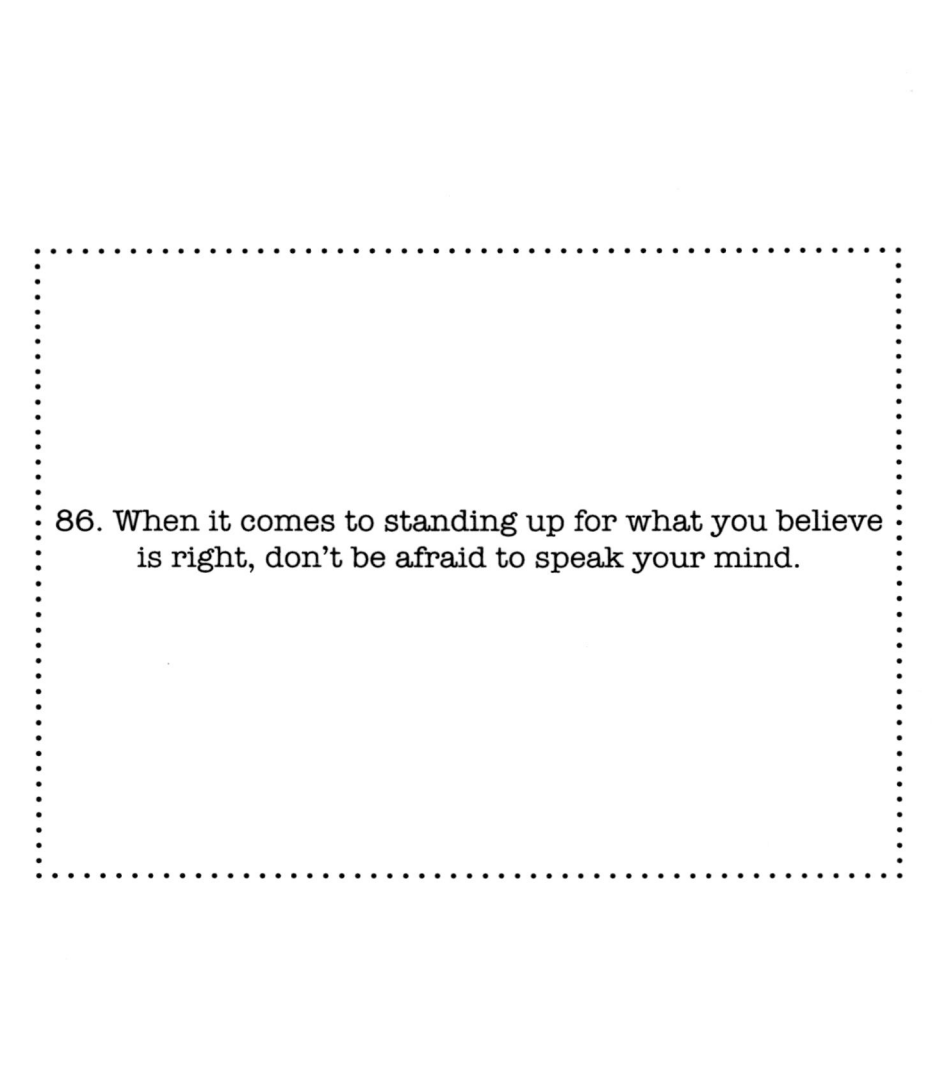

86. When it comes to standing up for what you believe is right, don't be afraid to speak your mind.

87. Instead of e-mailing a good friend, write an actual letter and mail it.

88. Live beneath your means. Get in the habit of saving 20 percent of your income and giving at least 5 percent to a charity that you believe in.

89. Be an example by actions, not words.

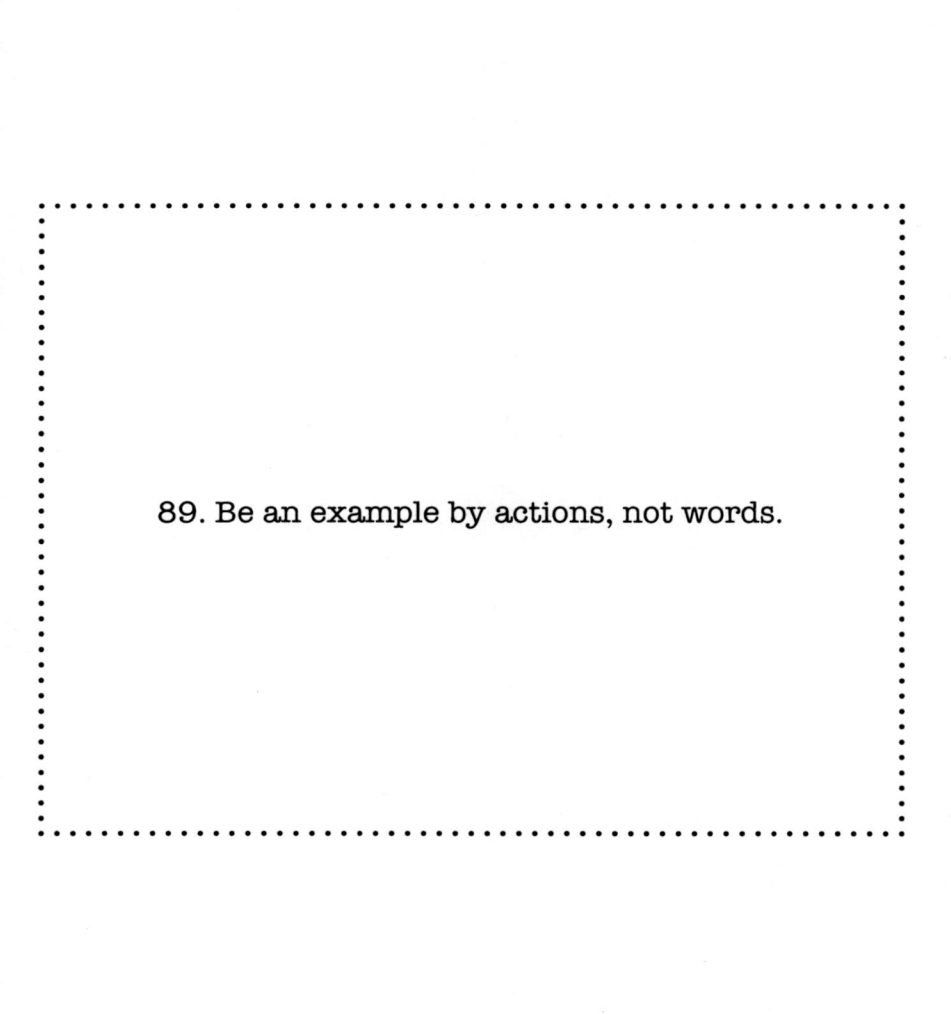

90. Anonymously donate money to a good cause.

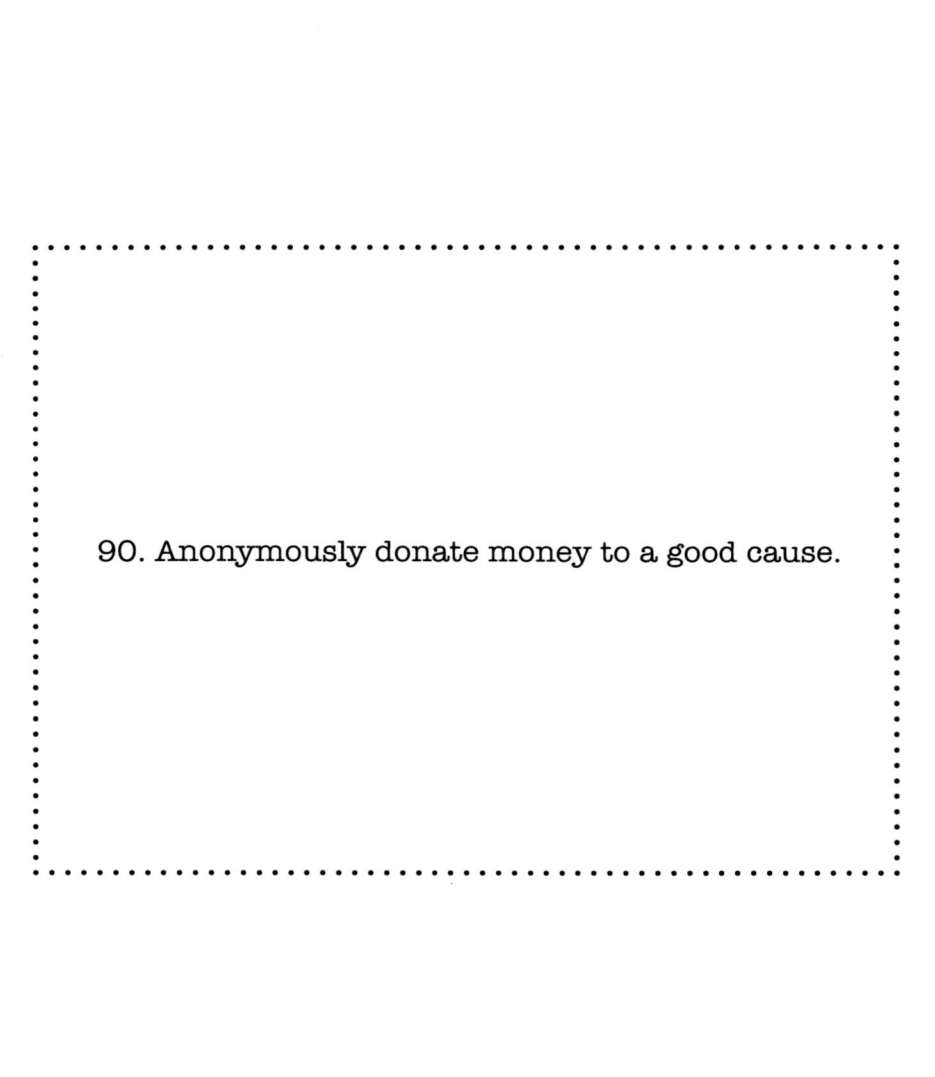

91. Pay the toll for the stranger behind you.

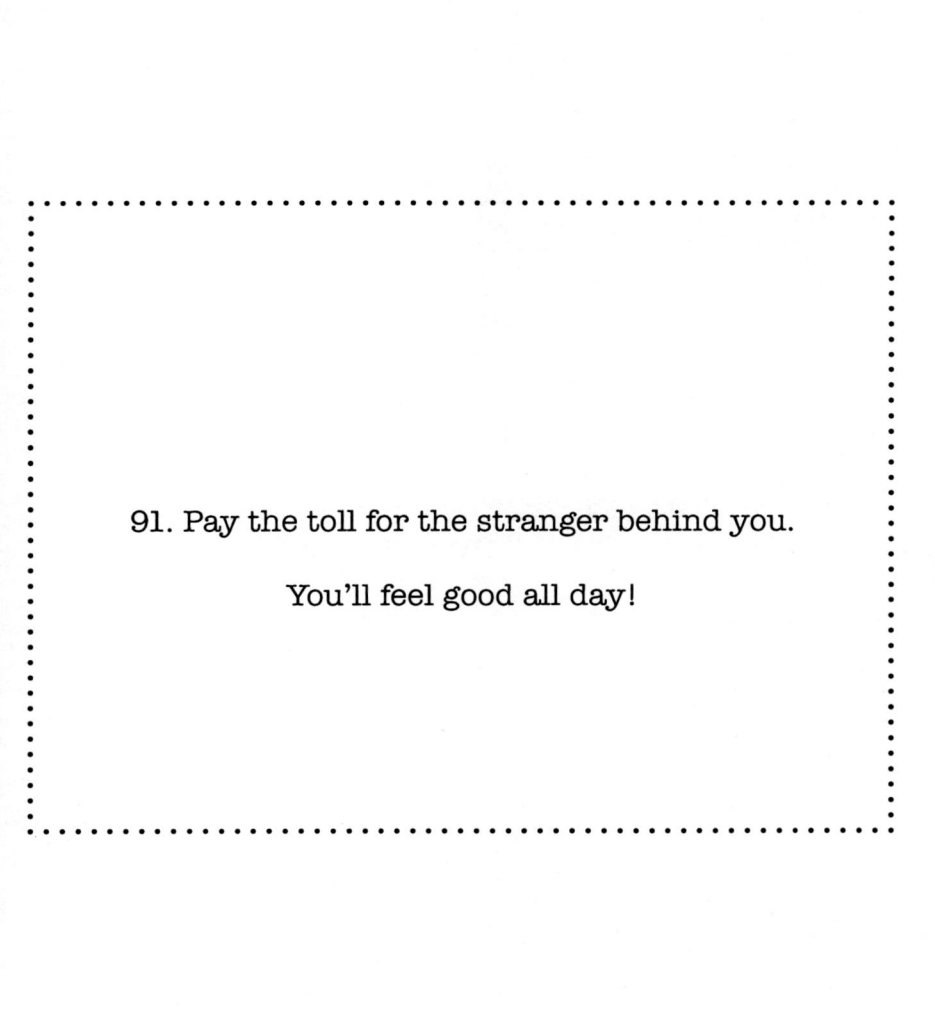

You'll feel good all day!

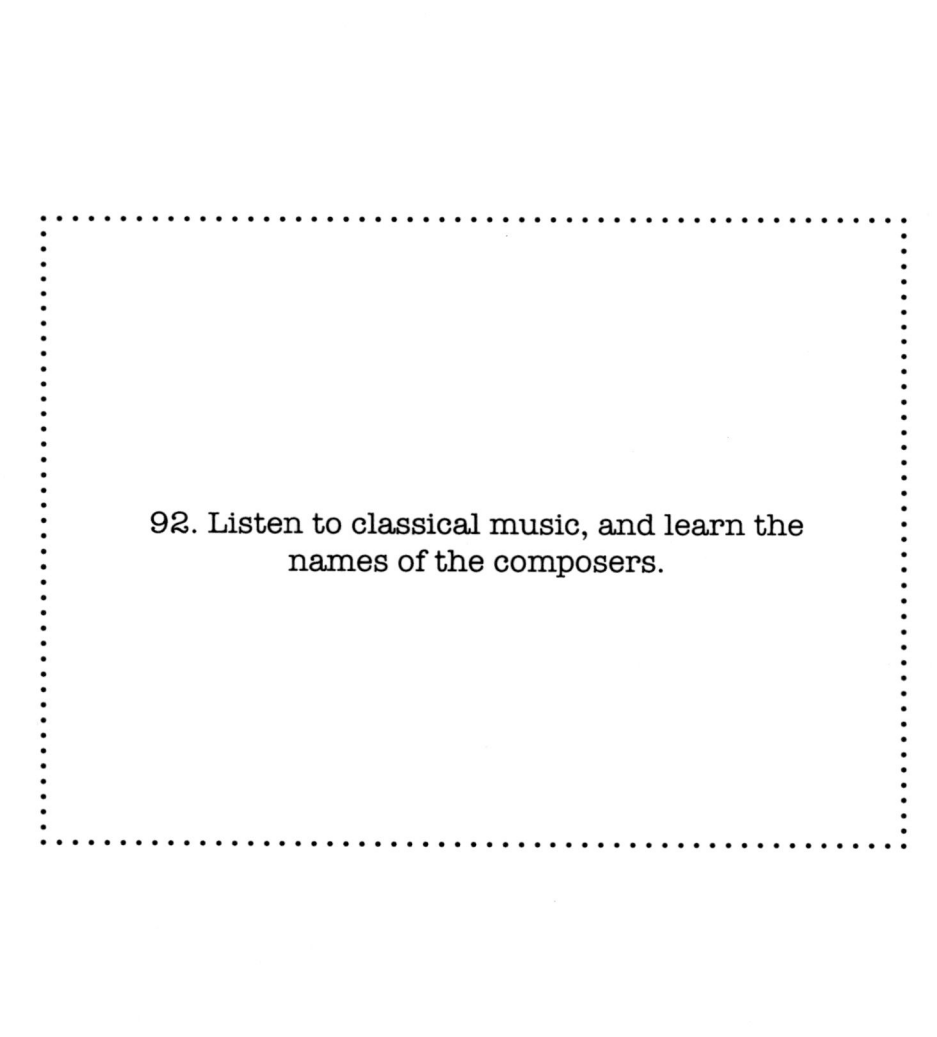

92. Listen to classical music, and learn the names of the composers.

93. Go to an opera.

94. Travel to another country and talk to the locals. Ask them sincerely curious questions about their culture and customs.

95. Write a letter to the president of the United States and express your opinion about his handling of a current event.

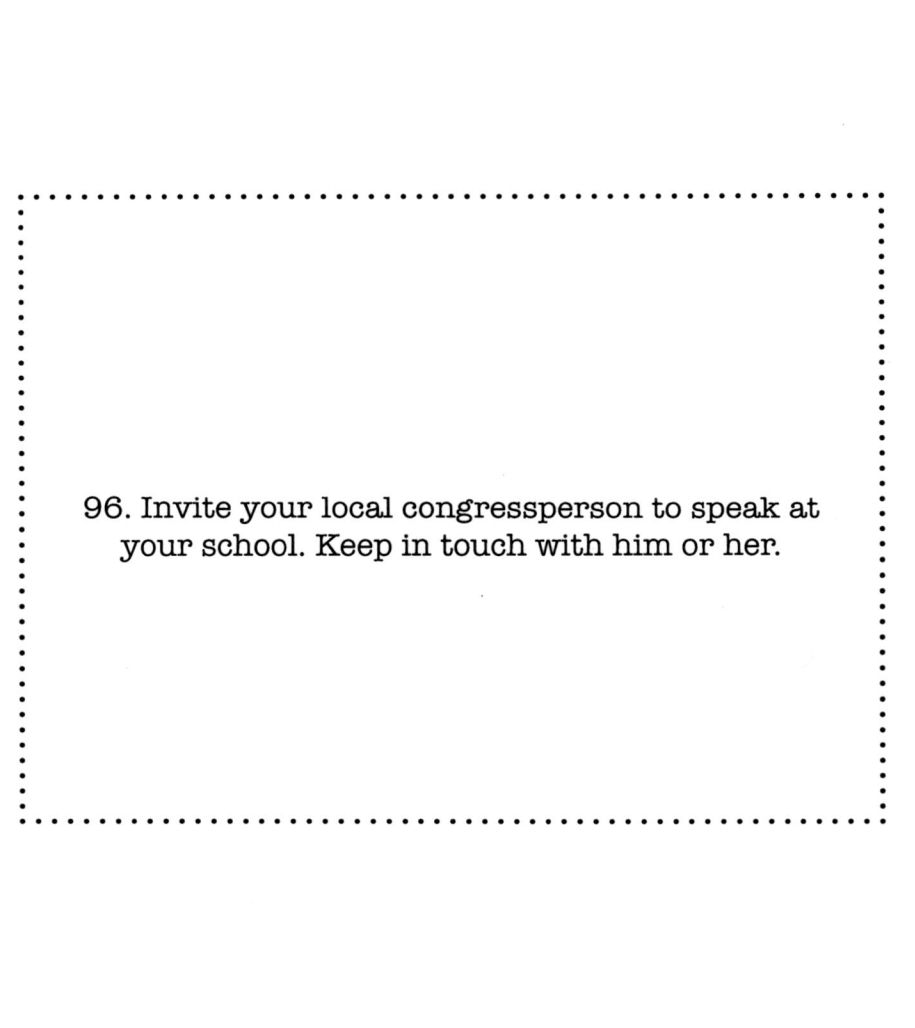

96. Invite your local congressperson to speak at your school. Keep in touch with him or her.

97. Clip coupons.

98. Pay off your credit card bills in full and right away when they come in.

Never buy something that you can't pay for right away, except a house or a car.

99. Set amazingly high goals for yourself.
The kind of goals that when people hear them,
they say, "Oh yeah, like that can
happen. Whatever."

Call them to say hello when
you've reached the goal.

100. Think for yourself.

Be proud, and don't let anyone else decide who you are and what you believe in.

101. Read this book once a year for the
rest of your life.

About the Author

As founder of NextStepU, David Mammano loves helping youth plan their futures. David grew NextStepU from its headquarters in Rochester, N.Y., to a publication and Web site with national distribution. NextStepU now reaches more than 4 million students, parents and counselors at more than 20,500 high schools in the United States.

At NextStepU.com, students can access articles, search for colleges and chat about planning for college.

David graduated from the University at Buffalo in 1991 with a degree in communications/advertising. David enjoys traveling, cooking, and spending time with his wife, Luisa, and kids, Gianluca and Melania, who will hopefully become outstanding young adults!

About NextStepU

NextStepU
Helping students find the right path.

David C. Mammano founded Next Step in 1995 out of his Rochester, N.Y., apartment. David's goal was to help students in his hometown get a grip on life after high school.

The magazine and Web site now reach more than 4 million readers in 20,500 high schools.

NextStepU covers college, careers and life. Our goal is to help high school juniors and seniors make educated decisions about their futures. We present the options; you decide your path.

Pick up a free copy of NextStepU Magazine from your high school guidance counselor's office, or check out NextStepU.com.